The Butterfly Arithmetic

The Butterfly Arithmetic

Irina Tyk

Civitas: Institute for the Study of Civil Society
London

Registered Charity No. 1085494

First Published December 2011

Text © Irina Tyk 2011

Illustrations and layout © Civitas

Published by
Civitas
55 Tufton Street
London SW1P 3QL

Civitas is a registered charity (no. 1085494)
and a company limited by guarantee, registered in
England and Wales (no. 04023541)

email: books@civitas.org.uk

ISBN 978-1-903386-60-6

Independence: The Institute for the Study of Civil Society (Civitas) is a registered educational charity (No. 1085494) and a company limited by guarantee (No. 04023541). Civitas is financed from a variety of private sources to avoid over-reliance on any single or small group of donors.

All publications are independently refereed. All the Institute's publications seek to further its objective of promoting the advancement of learning. The views expressed are those of the authors, not of the Institute.

Designed and typeset by Richard Kelly
Illustrations by Ed Dovey

Printed in Great Britain by
Berforts Group Ltd
Stevenage, SG1 2BH

'The science of numbers; the art of computation.'

Samuel Johnson

A Dictionary of the English Language, 1755

Contents

About the author

Irina Tyk is an honours graduate of the University of London. She has lectured at the University of Wales and the University of St. Andrews. Presently she is the Headmistress of Holland House School, an independent preparatory school.

She believes in the intellectual development of very young children in the structured environment of whole-class teaching. She believes that, after one year at school, children should be able to read independently. She continues to present these views on television and in public debate.

Irina Tyk was a director of The Butterfly Project from 1991 to 2009 which ran summer courses for children who wished to benefit from a rational and purposeful teaching approach.

Her phonics-based reading and writing course *The Butterfly Book* was published by Civitas in 2007 and its sequel and companion volume *The Butterfly Grammar* in 2008.

Introduction

For most of us, the language of numbers is universal. Unlike the language of words, the language of numbers traverses national boundaries and different expressions of culture. Like all languages that are not native to the speaker, the language of numbers must be learned. This is the purpose of *The Butterfly Arithmetic*: to teach children the language of numbers.

The degree to which the mind is shaped by its familiarity with numbers was brought home to me when I recently learned of a small Amazonian community whose language of numbers is restricted to 'around one', 'some' and 'many'. What profound differences of mind must there be when plurality is so limited!

In writing this book, I have been mindful of a child's need to acquire a numerical dexterity that will facilitate both the day-to-day conduct of his or her life and will also promote a rational education based on the logical principles of arithmetic and mathematics. Just as proficiency of language is not reliant on the perpetual use of a dictionary, so proficiency in the language of numbers is not reliant on the perpetual use of a calculator. Purposefully, *The Butterfly Arithmetic* omits entirely the use of calculators. One does not learn arithmetic from calculators!

Furthermore, this book eschews philosophic explanations for the concepts of number. Just as learning to read has nothing to do with William Empson's *Seven Levels of Ambiguity*, so learning to count and perform the four functions of arithmetic has nothing to do with Bertrand Russell's *Principia Mathematica*. Let the child first master the language of numbers before, if so inclined, he or she ponders the meaning of numbers at a much later stage of mental development. One thing is certain: deprive a child of the rudiments of the language of numbers and he or she will see less, will know less and will have the narrowest understanding of the world's plurality.

Irina Tyk
Holland House School
December 2011

How to make best use of this book

- This book may be used with any child who is deemed ready to learn to read and count. That is to say, most four- or five-year-olds may be taught about numbers by use of this book. It is not necessary that a child be able to read in order to learn from this book so long as a parent or teacher reads and explains the appropriate instructions.

- This is not a workbook, and so all written exercises should be completed in a separate exercise book. Many of the exercises may be completed orally.

- Initially, squared paper (with squares that are large enough to house a numeral) should be provided for the young child. Only when he or she is accustomed to working in columns may squared paper give way to lined paper.

- This course is an attempt to demystify what may appear to the young child as a maze of numbers whose relationship with one another is unclear. Just as the child must learn that knowledge is knowable, so he or she must learn that the language of numbers may be mastered.

- Each chapter of this book follows a carefully considered sequence. Therefore, the book should be used in the order in which it is set out. Of course, there will be times when a student may need to refer to specific chapters to correct an omission or to refresh some aspect of the language of numbers that requires clarification.

- This book may be used in the classroom or at home.

- The importance of mental arithmetic cannot be overstated. Arithmetical tables must be as embedded as the decoding of language. Ideally, children should commit to memory the arithmetical tables up to the $12\times$ table since some aspects of daily life, notably time, are subject to imperial measurement.

- Mental arithmetic should not be confined to arithmetical tables alone. Children must acquire a 'map' of number bonds that can be easily and quickly recalled, and that fix in the mind of a child relationships and connections between numbers. Proficiency in mental arithmetic is best acquired by the habit of practice for a short time every day.

- Visual cues have no place in mental arithmetic. The child who is counting by fingers, number lines, straws and other such visual aids cannot be said to be 'at home' with mental arithmetic.

- Numbers are not concretes. Like adjectives, they may be attached to concretes. The number 5 is not a concrete, but 5 dogs 'qualifies' the dogs by number. Number bonds reduce the unimaginable to the imaginable, so that one may not be able to imagine 1000 pencils but one may imagine 10 lots of 100 pencils. Likewise, to the inexperienced mathematician, 20 may be better understood as 2 groups of 10 or 4 groups of 5. That is to say, the language of numbers allows the child to know more than he can see.

- There is no reason why the more advanced child should not extend his or her proficiency to include larger and larger numbers.

- It is essential that all calculations that cannot be performed with ease without writing anything down are set out in columns. The concept of place value, whereby the same numeral stands for a different number according to the column in which it is placed, is an essential arithmetical tool. There are conventions and formalities of presentation that must be learned. Since arithmetic and mathematics are subjects of logic, the logic of how one arrives at the answer should not be concealed.

- The 'equals' sign is commonly misunderstood. It means 'the same as'; it does not necessarily signify the answer.

- Such terms as altogether, total, more than, less than, bigger and smaller should be understood aurally and, once he or she can read, in written form. Likewise, it is important that a child recognises the different terms that denote addition and subtraction: plus, minus, subtract, take away, etc.

- Speed is important. Numbers should be recognised quickly and written down with increasing fluency. Children should be encouraged to spread out their work rather than squash it up.

- The concept of plurality implies a commonality that is shared by more than one entity. If one intends to add or subtract animals or four-legged creatures, one may add cats and dogs; however, one cannot add cats and dogs in terms of either cats or dogs. Hence, the child should learn what may and may not be added together.

- This is not a theoretical work that seeks to cover every variation of arithmetic. The subject is set out in broad but specific categories to facilitate the learning process.

- Nothing in this book needs or should invite the use of a calculator.

Arithmetic is fun!

✿ LESSON **ONE** ✿

Introduce the names of the numbers **1** to **5**. On the presumption that the pupil is still unable to read, these numbers will be introduced by giving a name to each numeral; at this stage the number **1** will be identified by its name 'one', the number **2** by its name 'two', the number **3** by its name 'three', the number **4** by its name 'four' and the number **5** by its name 'five'. The pupil is not required to write the name of the number in letters. The numbers **1** to **5** must be memorised in sequence and must be identified out of sequence.

1. **Read out the following numbers:**

    1, 2, 3, 4, 5

    1, 1, 4, 3, 2, 2, 4, 5, 1, 5

    3, 5, 4, 2, 1, 4, 5, 2, 1, 3

    2, 2, 2, 5, 4, 5, 5, 1, 1, 3

    5, 4, 4, 3, 2, 1, 2, 3, 4, 5

2. **Listen to these numbers and write them down as numerals:**

    one, two, three, four, five

    two, two, five, four, four, three, three, one, one, three

five, four, three, two, one, four, three, five, two, one

Note: it is important that numbers are written correctly from top down and from left to right, and that the numbers can be written at a reasonable speed.

four, one, three, five, two, five, three, one, four, five

five, four, three, two, one

❧ LESSON **TWO** ❧

Introduce the concept whereby the number **1** stands for a single entity, which may be concrete as in **1** elephant or abstract as in **1** imaginary elephant. Likewise, introduce the numbers **2** to **5** whereby each number stands for real or imaginary entities.

The number **1** is unique in referring specifically to entities in the singular, whereas the numbers **2** to **5**, and all other numbers, refer to entities in the plural.

Introduce the concept of 'more than'. For example, the number **2** is one more than the number **1**; the number **3** is one more than the number **2**; the number **4** is one more than the number **3** and the number **5** is one more than the number **4**.

More advanced pupils may now be acquainted with the fact that the number **5** is not only one more than the number **4**; it is also two more than the number **3**, three more than the number **2** and four more than the number **1**. In the same way, the numbers **4**, **3** and **2** may be considered in relation to the concept of 'more than' [see LESSON SIX].

1. **Write down the number 1 and the number that is one more than 1.**

2. **Write down the number 2 and the number that is one more than 2.**

3. **Write down the number 3 and the number that is one more than 3.**

4. **Write down the number 4 and the number that is one more than 4.**

❧ LESSON **THREE** ❧

Introduce the questions: **'How many?'** and **'How many more?'**

- How many pencils can you see on the desk? Five (written as **5**).

- I have three blue pencils and one red pencil. How many pencils do I have altogether? Four (written as **4**). How many more of the pencils are blue rather than red? Two (written as **2**).

Note: the term that often appears in arithmetic, **'altogether'**, should now be introduced. It means: the total, the sum of everything that is added together. The fact that all the exercises at this stage are oral is deliberate in order to consolidate simple number bonds before the child learns to add or subtract.

Answer aloud:

a. **How many hands do you have, how many feet, how many heads, how many ears, how many fingers on one hand?**

b. **If you have 2 hats at home and 1 hat at school, how many more hats do you have at home?**

c. Ponti has 3 woolly jumpers in his bedroom. He has 2 in his bathroom cupboard. How many woolly jumpers does Ponti have altogether? How many more of his woolly jumpers are in his bedroom?

d. 2 children are playing in the garden and 5 children are playing in the kitchen. How many more are playing in the kitchen?

e. There are 5 elephants in the zoo. One is sitting on a tree trunk and the other 4 are bathing in the pond. How many more are bathing in the pond?

f. Your pet monkey, Blinchik, has eaten 3 bananas. You gave him 5 bananas at breakfast time. How many more has he still to eat before there are no bananas left for him to eat?

g. If there are 4 cars zooming along the road and there are 2 cars parked on the grass, how many more cars are zooming along the road?

Note: introduce the meaning of 'fewer' and 'less than' as in 'Are there fewer or more? How many fewer? Is three more or less than four?'

h. If I can see 1 duck on the pavement and 4 ducks in the pond, are there more ducks on the pavement or in the pond? How many more? Are there fewer ducks on the pavement or in the pond? How many fewer?

i. Now write down the following numbers: three, five, four, one, two, two, three, five, four, one, one more than three, two more than two, three more than two, two less than three, four less than five, one less than two, four more than one, one more than one.

❧ LESSON **FOUR** ❧

Introduce the names of the numbers **6** to **9**. On the presumption that the pupil is still unable to read, these numbers will be introduced by giving a name to each numeral; at this stage the number **6** will be identified by its name 'six', the number **7** by its name 'seven', the number **8** by its name 'eight', the number **9** by its name 'nine'. The pupil is <u>not</u> required to write the name of the number in letters. The numbers **6** to **9** must be memorised in sequence and must be identified out of sequence.

1. **Read the following numbers:**

   6, 7, 8, 9, 1, 2, 3, 4, 5

   1, 2, 3, 4, 5, 6, 7, 8, 9

   5, 8, 3, 7, 8, 4, 2, 6, 4, 7

   7, 9, 9, 8, 4, 6, 5, 1, 1, 8

   9, 8, 7, 6, 5, 4, 3, 2, 1, 2

2. **Listen to these numbers and write them down as numerals:**

   one, two, three, four, five, six, seven, eight, nine, six, two, five, nine, four, eight, six, three, one, one, five, four, three, two, one, nine, eight, seven, six, two, four, one, eight, six, two, nine,

three, five, four, three, nine, seven, five, three, one, two, four, six, eight, nine

3. **Answer aloud:**

    a. **You have 3 woolly scarves at home. Mum has 4 woolly scarves. How many do you and mum have altogether?**

    b. **4 puppies are playing in the park. 3 more puppies join them. How many puppies are now playing in the park?**

    c. **Annie sings beautifully. She sang 2 songs at her party and was asked to sing 1 more. How many songs did she sing altogether?**

    d. **There are 6 pictures on the wall. The teacher puts 2 more pictures on the wall. How many pictures are there on the wall altogether?**

    e. **Sabrina has 3 red pencils. Her sister, Mandy, has 8 red pencils. Who has more red pencils? How many more?**

f. Oliver goes to the zoo and sees 3 monkeys playing on a swing. 5 monkeys are sitting on a branch. How many monkeys does Oliver see altogether?

g. Trudi writes 3 letters to her mum. The next day, she writes 4 more letters. How many letters does Trudi write altogether?

h. Frankie is putting flowers into a vase. She puts 5 roses into the vase and then adds 3 daffodils. How many flowers are in the vase altogether?

i. On Tuesday, Fred ate 2 sandwiches. On Wednesday, he ate 3 sandwiches, and on Thursday he ate 4 sandwiches. How many sandwiches did he eat on Tuesday and Wednesday? How many sandwiches did he eat on Tuesday and Thursday? How many sandwiches did he eat altogether on Tuesday, Wednesday and Thursday?

❧ LESSON **FIVE** ❧

Revise 'more than' and 'less than' using the numbers **1** to **9**.

EXAMPLE

- **6** is **1** more than **5**.
- **7** is **2** more than **5**.
- **8** is **3** more than **5**.
- **7** is **2** less than **9**.
- **6** is **3** less than **9**.

Note: children should be taught to use 'less' and 'fewer' correctly. One speaks of 'three is <u>less</u> than four' but 'he has <u>fewer</u> toys than his sister'. 'Less' is a comparative adverb (little, less, least) and 'fewer' is a comparative adjective (few, fewer, fewest).

1. **Write down how many legs a spider has, how many legs an octopus has, how many legs an elephant has and, if you do not count your thumbs, how many fingers you have on both hands.**

2. **If you have 9 pencils at home and 6 pencils at school, how many more pencils do you have at home?**

3. **My puppy, Hamlet, has hidden 8 bones under the garden bench. He has 2 more under his bed. How many fewer bones**

does he have under his bed? How many more bones does he have under the garden bench?

4. 7 kittens are playing in the back garden and 3 kittens are playing in the front garden. How many more are playing in the back garden?

5. There are 9 giraffes in the zoo. 6 are standing near some trees and the other 3 are drinking from the stream. How many fewer giraffes are having a drink rather than standing near some trees?

6. Your pet monkey, Topsy, can now climb 8 branches of the tall tree in the garden. Last week Topsy could only climb 2 branches. How many more branches can he now climb?

7. Before school there were 6 children in the playground. At lunch time there were only 2 children in the playground. How many more children were there in the playground before school than at lunch time?

8. **If I can see 9 cars outside the shop and 5 cars parked outside my house, how many fewer cars are parked outside my house?**

9. **Write down the following numbers: nine, five, three, eight, seven, four, six, seven, five, one, one more than seven, two more than six, three more than two, two less than eight, four less than nine, one less than two, six more than three, one more than two.**

❧ LESSON **SIX** ❧

Introduce addition, denoted by a plus sign (**+**). Addition allows numbers to be increased by specific amounts; it is the means by which one number is combined with another number to create a higher number. At this stage, addition will be restricted to those numbers that the pupil has already learned: namely, the numbers **1** to **9**.

Addition is expressed by the use of the '**+** sign' as in:
* **1 + 1** makes **2**.
* **1 + 1 + 1** makes **3**.
* **1 + 1 + 1 + 1 + 1 + 1 + 1 + 1 + 1** makes **9**.

There are various ways of adding numbers:
* **1 + 6** makes **7**.
* **2 + 5** makes **7**.
* **3 + 4** makes **7**.
* **1 + 1 + 1 + 1 + 1 + 1 + 1** makes **7**.
* **2 + 1 + 1 + 1 + 1 + 1** makes **7**.
* **3 + 1 + 1 + 1 + 1** makes **7**.
* **4 + 1 + 1 + 1** makes **7**.
* **5 + 1 + 1** makes **7**.
* **2 + 2 + 2 + 1** makes **7**.
* **3 + 3 + 1** makes **7**.
* **4 + 2 + 1** makes **7**.
* And so on.

It is important that children learn that changing the order of numbers has no effect on the outcome so that **1 + 3** is the same as **3 + 1**.

The more children see different combinations of numbers that may be added together to make another number the better. Needless to say, the lower the number the fewer the combinations, the higher the number the more combinations there are.

1. **Write down the plus sign.**

2. **What do the following numbers add up to:**

    1 + 4,   5 + 3,   4 + 2,   8 + 1,   6 + 2

    4 + 3,   1 + 8,   7 + 2,   2 + 7,   3 + 6

    1 + 1 + 2,   1 + 1 + 3,   2 + 1 + 2,

    2 + 3 + 3,   4 + 1 + 2

    6 + 1 + 1,   2 + 5 + 1,   3 + 2 + 1,

    1 + 1 + 7,   5 + 2 + 2

    1 + 2 + 3 + 2,   2 + 2 + 2 + 2,

    3 + 4 + 1 + 1

    5 + 1 + 2 + 1,   6 + 1 + 1 + 1,

    2 + 3 + 3 + 1

3. **Write down the different ways to make the number 6 by using the plus sign.**

4. **Write down the different ways to make the number 5 by using the plus sign.**

5. Write down the different ways to make the number 9 by using the plus sign.

6. Ponti has 3 lollipops. He buys 3 more lollipops. Use the plus sign to add the lollipops and write down how many lollipops Ponti has now.

7. I see 5 cars in the car park. 2 more cars arrive. Use the plus sign to add together the number of cars there are now in the car park.

8. Blinchik is sitting on the fence and counting the branches on a tree. He counts 5 and then adds 4 more. Write down how many branches he sees on the tree.

9. Bob has 3 marbles in his pocket, 2 marbles in his hand and 1 marble which has fallen onto the floor. How many marbles does Bob have altogether?

❦ LESSON **SEVEN** ❦

Introduce the equals sign (**=**). 'Equals' means 'the same as'. The number 'one' is the same as the number 'one' as in **1 = 1**, **1 + 1 = 2** and **2 = 1 + 1**.

1 + 1 + 1 = 3
1 + 2 = 3

or,

3 = 1 + 1 + 1
3 = 1 + 2

Note: **'equals' does <u>not</u> mean 'the answer'.**

1. Do these:

a. **Write down the 'equals' sign.**

b. **Write down the 'plus' sign.**

c. **What does 4 add 3 equal?**

d. **What does 2 add 7 equal?**

e. **What does 5 add 3 equal?**

f. **What does 6 add 2 equal?**

g. **What does 1 add 7 equal?**

h. **What does 3 add 4 equal?**

i. **What does 7 add 1 equal?**

2. **Now do these:**

    a. **What equals 3 add 2?**

    b. **What equals 5 add 1?**

    c. **What equals 8 add 1?**

    d. **What equals 2 add 4?**

    e. **What equals 4 add 5?**

    f. **What does the word 'equals' mean?**

3. **Write down the following sums and insert the correct answers in the space provided:**

    a. $1 + 8 = \dots$

    b. $4 + 3 = \dots$

    c. $\dots = 6 + 2$

    d. $\dots = 2 + 5$

    e. $3 + 6 = \dots$

    f. $\dots = 4 + 2$

    g. $\dots = 2 + 2 + 1$

    h. $6 + 2 + 1 = \dots$

    i. $3 + 3 + 2 = \dots$

4. Lucy painted 3 colours of the rainbow. There are 7 colours in the rainbow. How many more must she paint if she wants all 7 colours in her picture?

5. What number equals 6 add 3?

6. How many different ways can you make the number 4? The number 5? The number 6? The number 7?

7. One day, Ben looks out of the window and sees 3 flower pots. 2 days later, he looks out of the window and sees 4 more flower pots. If he adds all the pots together, how many flower pots can he see?

8. Sam collects toy cars. He has 6 cars in his toy box. On his birthday, he was given 3 more cars. How many cars does Sam now have?

9. There are 5 pencils in the pot. Pam adds 2 more. How many pencils are there in the pot now?

❧ LESSON **EIGHT** ❧

Introduce the symbol **0** that on its own stands for nothing; that is to say it denotes neither a positive nor a negative value. Adding nought to any number will not increase it or decrease it. For reasons of spelling and pronunciation, many prefer 'zero' to 'nought'.

Introduce the number **10**, the first two-digit number that follows the number **9**. Now it is appropriate to explain that our numerical system contains no numerals greater than **9**. The whole number (integer) that follows **9** is denoted by one set of ten and no set of units. It is written in two columns: **10**.

Note: children may now discover that the numerals **1** to **9** may be placed in the units column to denote one set of numbers and in the tens column to denote another set of numbers. This is the basis of our positional system of numbering; it allows the child to move from precepts, that are relatively few in number as in ten fingers, to concepts that are many in number and are beyond perceptual restriction. Hence, one only needs the numerals **1** to **9** to denote any number of any magnitude.

1. **Read and write down the numbers 1 to 10.**

2. **Write down nought.**

3. **Which number is 4 more than 5?**

4. **Which number is 4 less than 5?**

5. **Which number is 1 more than 9?**

6. **Which number is 1 less than 9?**

7. **Which number is 2 less than 10?**

8. **Which number is 5 less than 10?**

9. **Which number is the same as 5 add 5?**

10. **Which number equals 4 add 4?**

11. **Write down the following sums and the correct answers in the space provided:**

> a. $0 + 0 + 0 = $ .....
>
> b. $0 + 1 = $ .....
>
> c. $1 + 0 = $ .....
>
> d. $10 + 0 = $ .....
>
> e. $9 + 1 = $ .....
>
> f. ..... $= 1 + 9$
>
> g. ..... $= 5 + 5$
>
> h. $2 + 7 = $ .....
>
> i. $2 + 8 = $ .....
>
> j. $1 + 2 + 3 = $ .....

12. Now do these:

a. $1 + 2 + 3 + 4 = $ .....

b. ..... $= 2 + 2 + 4$

c. ..... $= 3 + 3 + 4$

d. $3 + 0 + 1 = $ .....

e. $4 + 1 + 5 = $ .....

f. $4 + 3 + 2 + 1 = $ .....

g. $0 + 0 + 0 + 0 + 0 + 0 + 1 = $ .....

h. $1 + 0 + 1 + 0 + 1 + 0 + 0 = $ .....

i. ..... $= 2 + 1 + 3 + 0 + 0 + 4$

j. $3 + $ ..... $= 2 + 6$

13. Write down the answers to the following:

a. 5 boys are sitting in the classroom. 5 more boys walk in and sit down. How many boys are now sitting in the classroom?

b. 4 girls are standing by the window. 6 girls are sitting by the door. How many girls are there altogether?

c. **7 zebras are galloping across the grass. 2 more zebras come. How many zebras are there now?**

d. **I have 3 oranges. My friend gives me 2 more. How many oranges do I have now?**

e. **Pinky has 3 toys. She is given 3 more toys on her birthday. How many toys does she have now?**

f. **Anton has 5 red pencils. His teacher gives him 3 green pencils. How many pencils does he have now?**

g. **There are 3 fish in the pond. Daddy adds 2 more fish. How many fish are now in the pond?**

h. **Mr Magoo loves clocks. He has a clock in every room of the house. There are 8 rooms altogether. How many clocks does Mr Magoo have?**

i. **There are 5 books on the teacher's desk. She adds 5 more books. How many books are now on her desk?**

j.   **Dogs have 4 legs. Noah sees 2 dogs in the park. How many legs do the two dogs have altogether?**

PONTI PANDA AND THE MATCHBOX

Late one evening, Ponti Panda decided to light a fire in the garden and sit by it until midnight. He wanted to enjoy the pleasant late summer evening.

He stood on tiptoe and reached for the top shelf of the kitchen cupboard where the matchbox was kept. He opened it rather too quickly and, of course, he dropped the box and all the matches fell out.

"Oh dear! Oh dear! What a clumsy bear am I!" exclaimed Ponti. "I must pick them up one by one, now."

He began to do so. He counted them one by one as he put them back in the matchbox. He counted up to ten using his ten fingers and then he stopped. He could not go on. What was he to do? He clenched his hands together into one fat ball. Inside were his ten fat fingers. He made ten into one lot of ten. He was very pleased with himself and thought he could begin to count again. The next number was a ball of ten

plus one extra. Such a number must have a name. But he did not know its name. And so Ponti had to learn about a new number which he found on the next page of this book.

❧ LESSON **NINE** ❧

Introduce the numbers **11** to **19**. These numbers are written with the digits **1** to **9** as units whereas the component of ten is indicated by the digit **1** that is placed on the left side of the digit denoting the number of units.

EXAMPLE

11 = 10 + 1

12 = 10 + 2

13 = 10 + 3, and so on.

1. Read out the following numbers:

10, 11, 12, 13, 14, 15, 16, 17, 18, 19

12, 11, 14, 15, 13, 12, 11, 18, 17, 13

19, 18, 11, 13, 17, 16, 15, 11, 10

9, 19, 7, 16, 8, 6, 17, 12, 8, 5, 15, 10, 4, 1, 12, 2, 11, 0, 10

19, 18, 17, 16, 15, 14, 13, 12, 11, 10, 9, 8, 7, 6, 5, 4, 3, 2, 1

2. **Listen to these numbers and write them down as numerals:**

> ten, eleven, twelve, thirteen, fourteen, fifteen, sixteen, seventeen, eighteen, nineteen

> thirteen, eleven, fifteen, five, three, eighteen, six, nought, ten, three

> four, fourteen, sixteen, one, four, seven, eleven, ten, nought, one

3. **Write down the number thirteen and the number that is one less than thirteen.**

4. **Write down the number nineteen and the number that is two less than nineteen.**

5. **Write down nought and the next three numbers after nought; now write down the number ten and the next four numbers after ten.**

6. **Choose two of the following numbers to add together to give 18:**

> **7, 9, 11, 13, 15, 17**

7. **Write down the numbers between 9 and 19.**

8. **Write down the number that is 4 more than 11.**

9. **What equals 9 add 10?**

10. **What equals 0 add 13?**

❦ LESSON **TEN** ❦

Revision: the following sums should be written out in a separate book and the correct answers should be placed where indicated.

Write down the following sums and insert the correct answers in the space provided:

a. $3 + 8 =$ .....

b. $5 + 4 =$ .....

c. $4 + 9 =$ .....

d. $8 + 10 =$ .....

e. $5 + 10 =$ .....

f. $2 + 10 =$ .....

g. $0 + 19 =$ .....

h. $7 + 9 =$ .....

i. $8 + 7 =$ .....

j. $14 + 3 =$ .....

k. ..... $= 5 + 4$

l. ..... $= 3 + 8$

m. ..... = 6 + 11

n. ..... = 7 + 12

o. ..... = 4 + 14

p. ..... = 0 + 0

q. 1 + 11 + 4 = ...

r. 4 + 4 + 11 = ...

s. 7 + 0 + 9 = ...

t. ..... = 0 + 10 + 6

✿ LESSON **ELEVEN** ✿

Although the following problems should be given orally, children ought to write down the appropriate sum followed by the answer; that is to say, children should write down the numbers with the appropriate operational sign (**+**), followed by the equals sign (**=**).

1. **Ponti decides to paint his room blue. He paints 1 wall and likes it very much. If his room has 4 walls, how many more walls does he have to paint?**

2. **Jodi saw 6 ducks swimming in the pond. 8 more ducks jumped in. How many ducks are in the pond now?**

3. **Frank ate 6 lollipops. A little later, he ate 4 more lollipops and 1 piece of fruit. How many lollipops did he eat altogether?**

4. **Grandma bought 16 packets of crisps. She forgot that there were 19 children coming to the party. How many more packets should she buy so that every child has one packet?**

5. **Pinky and Fran go shopping. They buy 6**

apples and 9 pears. How many pieces of fruit did they buy?

6. Ponti has 11 black pencils. His best friend gives him a box of 7 pencils. How many pencils does Ponti have now?

7. Fat Sam loves chocolates. He ate 6 chocolates on Tuesday, 4 on Wednesday, 3 on Thursday and 4 on Friday.

   a. How many chocolates did he eat on Tuesday and Wednesday?

   b. How many chocolates did he eat on Thursday and Friday?

   c. How many chocolates did he eat on Tuesday and Friday?

   d. How many chocolates did he eat altogether?

8. Fat Sam decided that he must lose weight and so he went on a diet. In January he lost 3 pounds. In February he lost 4 pounds. In March he lost 6 pounds. How many pounds did he lose altogether?

9. Aunty Meg buys 3 balloons for Katrina's party. Then she remembered that Katrina wanted 6 balloons so Aunty Meg bought 3 more balloons plus an extra 1 just in case a balloon popped accidentally. How many balloons did she buy altogether?

10. Buttons is a very jolly puppy. He loves jelly beans. Yesterday he ate 5 jelly beans. Today, he was a very naughty dog and pinched 6 more jelly beans when no one was looking. How many jelly beans did he eat altogether?

PONTI PANDA DROPS HIS MARBLES

Ponti found it difficult to learn not to be clumsy. After all, he had rather fat soft paws. So, it was no surprise that he dropped his box of marbles. Unfortunately, it was rather a large box with twenty marbles inside.

When he dropped the marbles and they scattered all over the floor, Ponti decided to practise the new numbers that he had learned. He decided to count them as he picked the marbles up and put them back in the box. When there were nineteen marbles inside

the box, there was still one left over on the floor. The time had come to learn about the number that was one more than nineteen.

He knew that all the numbers that were higher than nine had two numbers. He knew that the number ten had a 'one' on the left and a 'nought' alongside it on the right. Each number was in a different column. He knew about columns. They were like tall blocks on buildings that stretched upwards. Sometimes long and narrow columns stood at the front entrances of buildings. Newspapers printed stories in columns and teachers wrote down the names of pupils in columns. Ponti could write numbers in columns in his exercise book, too. He knew that every number from 'ten' to 'nineteen' started with 'one' in the tens column. He wondered if the next number after 'nineteen' would start with a 'two' in the tens column. He was about to find out by turning to the next chapter.

He couldn't wait…

❧ LESSON **TWELVE** ❧

Revise the concept of **0** in Lesson Nine.

Introduce the number **20**. The number **20** is written in two columns; the first column denotes tens, the second column denotes units.

It is now appropriate to explain that not only can the digit **2** be placed in the tens column but so can the digits **3**, **4**, **5**, **6**, **7**, **8** & **9** to denote the larger numbers **30**, **40**, **50**, **60**, **70**, **80** & **90**.

Once children can recognise the numbers **10** and **20**, they can count up in tens: one lot of ten is **10**, two lots of ten are **20**, three lots of ten are **30**, and so on.

1. **Write down these numbers: nought, ten, twenty, nineteen, five, fifteen, six, seventeen, twenty.**

2. **Write down the number that comes after 2.**

3. **Write down the next two numbers after 8.**

4. **Write down the number which is 1 more than 10.**

5. **Write down the number which is 1 more than 13.**

6. Write down the number which is 3 more than 17.

7. Write down the number which is 2 less than 20.

8. Write down the number which is 1 less than 20.

9. Write down the number which is 4 more than 16.

10. Write down 5 different ways of adding 2 numbers to give 17.

11. Now do these:

   a. $2 + 10 =$

   b. $3 + 9 =$

   c. $6 + 13 =$

   d. $6 + 14 =$

   e. $8 + 12 =$

   f. $9 + 11 =$

   g. $0 + 19 =$

h. 0 + 20 =

i. 15 + 5 =

j. 8 + 4 + 8 =

k. ..... = 10 + 10

l. ..... = 2 + 12

m. ..... = 4 + 14

n. ..... = 8 + 8

o. ..... = 13 + 7

p. 10 + 3 =

q. 11 + 4 =

r. 10 + 10 =

s. 4 + 10 + 6 =

t. 19 + 1 =

12. **Now do these:**

a. **Write down 5 different addition sums, using only 2 numbers, to make 20.**

b. **What is 4 less than 20?**

c. **What is 7 more than 13?**

d. **20 birds landed on the grass. Afterwards, 10 more birds landed. How many birds were there on the grass altogether?**

e. **Danny collects stamps. He has 50 altogether. A few months later, he finds that he has another 40. How many stamps does he have altogether?**

f. **Nolita loves chocolates. She eats 10 chocolates on Monday, 2 chocolates on Tuesday, 10 chocolates on Wednesday and 20 chocolates on Thursday.**

   • **How many chocolates does she eat altogether on Monday and Thursday?**

   • **How many chocolates does she eat altogether on Tuesday and Wednesday?**

- How many chocolates does she eat altogether on Monday, Tuesday and Wednesday?

- How many chocolates does she eat altogether on all four days?

13. Pepita likes to draw circles. Yesterday she drew 10 circles in her book. Today she added another 20 circles and tomorrow she will draw 10 more. How many circles will she have in her book after tomorrow?

14. What equals 10 add 10?

15. What equals 5 add 6 add 7?

16. Write down:

   a. 4 more than 20

   b. 6 less than 20

   c. 8 more than 22

   d. 5 more than 24

❧ LESSON **THIRTEEN** ❧

Revision of the numbers **10**, **20**, **30**, **40**, **50**, **60**, **70**, **80** and **90**.

1. **Read out the following numbers:**

    11, 12, 13, 14, 15, 16, 17, 18, 19, 20

    10, 20, 30, 40, 50, 60, 70, 80, 90

    1, 2, 3, 4, 5, 6, 7, 8, 9, 10

    3, 30, 4, 40, 5, 50, 6, 60, 7, 70, 8, 80, 9, 90

    14, 6, 60, 13, 70, 4, 90, 0, 10, 20

2. **Listen to these numbers and write them down as numerals:**

    Five, fifty, thirteen, nineteen, ninety, eighty, eleven, nought

    four, forty, ten, eight, seventy, six, four, nineteen, ten, two

    twenty, thirty, three, sixteen, six, sixty, seven, seventeen

3. **Write down the answers:**

a. **Jenny buys 7 packets of crisps. Nicki buys the same number of packets. They put all the packets into their mum's shopping bag. How many packets are there now in the shopping bag?**

b. **Rebecca wants to buy some balloons for her friends. She sees a packet of 10 balloons on the shelf. If she buys 2 packets, how many balloons will she have altogether?**

c. **There are 16 marbles in the bag. Priti finds 3 more marbles on the floor and adds them to the bag. How many marbles are there altogether in the bag?**

d. **Alex brings 13 stickers to school on Monday. On Tuesday, she buys 5 more stickers. How many stickers does she have altogether?**

e. **Sam puts 7 spoons into the**

dishwasher. He finds 8 more dirty spoons and puts them in the dishwasher too. How many spoons are there in the dishwasher altogether?

f. Angus collects toy cars. He has 3 yellow cars, 8 green cars and 2 black cars. He puts them on the shelf and counts them. Can you find out how many cars Angus has altogether on the shelf?

g. Adam loves fish and on Saturdays he goes to the pet shop to look at all the fish. There are 5 fish in one tank, 12 fish in another tank and 1 lonely fish on his own in a small fish tank. How many fish does Sam see altogether?

h. Sabrina likes to collect rubbers. She has 16 rubbers at school and 4 rubbers in her box at home. How many rubbers does she have altogether?

i. **Add 10 and 10. Then add another 10 to your answer. Don't forget your answer. Now add 20 to your answer. What number do you now have?**

j. **Add 20 and 30. Then add another 10 to your answer. Don't forget your answer. Now add 20 to your answer. What number do you now have?**

❧ LESSON **FOURTEEN** ❧

Introduce the setting out of numbers in tens and units columns as follows.

Instead of 2 + 4 = 6, write:

$$\begin{array}{r} 2 \\ +\ 4 \\ \hline 6 \\ \hline \end{array}$$

Instead of 2 + 10 = 12, write:

$$\begin{array}{r} 2 \\ +\ 10 \\ \hline 12 \\ \hline \end{array}$$

Instead of 10 + 20 = 30, write:

$$\begin{array}{r} 10 \\ +\ 20 \\ \hline 30 \\ \hline \end{array}$$

Note: at this stage, it is important to use squared paper, with squares of a reasonable size, so that children use squares to align columns and to keep numbers properly spaced out, neither too far away from one another nor too close to each other.

Furthermore, it is a good idea for children to learn how to draw a margin with a ruler on the left side of the page. This will be a valuable exercise in dexterity. The lines above and below the answer should also be drawn neatly with a ruler.

The following exercise – and all such exercises that follow – should be copied, by the child into an exercise book. As each sum is copied down, the child should write the answer down in the correct manner. The careful writing down of the numbers in straight columns is most important.

DO NOT ALLOW THE CHILD FIRST TO COPY ALL THE SUMS DOWN AND THEN WRITE IN THE ANSWERS.

a.
$$6$$
$$+\ 3$$
————

b.
$$4$$
$$+\ 5$$
————

c.
$$1$$
$$+\ 8$$
————

d.
$$2$$
$$+\ 5$$
————

e.
$$3$$
$$+\ 3$$
————

f.
$$7$$
$$+\ 1$$
————

g.
$$10$$
$$+\ 8$$
————

h.
$$3$$
$$+\ 10$$
————

i.
$$14$$
$$+\ 10$$
————

j.
$$10$$
$$+\ 10$$
————

k.
$$10$$
$$+\ 20$$
————

l.
$$30$$
$$+\ 10$$
————

m. 10
  + 30
  _____

n. 20
  + 20
  _____

o. 10
  + 40
  _____

p. 50
  + 10
  _____

q. 30
  + 30
  _____

r. 10
  + 60
  _____

s. 20
  + 40
  _____

t. 7
  + 70
  _____

❦ LESSON **FIFTEEN** ❦

Now children should learn to transpose sums that are written out horizontally into vertical columns.

EXAMPLE

6 + 4 =
$$\begin{array}{r} 6 \\ + 4 \\ \hline \\ \hline \end{array}$$

1. Write these sums out in columns and work out the correct answer.

     a. **3 + 4 =**

     b. **80 + 10 =**

     c. **10 + 2 =**

     d. **20 + 20 =**

     e. **60 + 10 =**

     f. **8 + 10 =**

     g. **30 + 30 =**

     h. **40 + 40 =**

     i. **10 + 6 =**

j. $50 + 40 =$

k. $3 + 10 =$

l. $5 + 10 =$

m. $60 + 10 =$

n. $10 + 40 =$

o. $10 + 60 =$

p. $10 + 40 =$

q. $10 + 20 =$

r. $9 + 10 =$

s. $30 + 60 =$

t. $40 + 50 =$

PONTI PANDA BUILDS A BRICK WALL

Ponti Panda was building a brick wall. He wanted to practise counting bricks. Building a brick wall was a good way of counting. He built the wall five bricks high which brought it to the level of his tummy. He could still jump over it. He added another five bricks and could barely see over the wall, but he did not want to stop building his brick wall. So he brought a ladder, climbed up and added more bricks, fifteen, twenty, thirty, forty, fifty and he sang along as he counted and climbed up and down, up and down the ladder. It was mid-afternoon and it was getting hotter and hotter. Ponti climbed down. He drank some lemonade and put on a Panama hat to keep his head cool. Then he started all over again. He huffed and he puffed. His ears burned and his nose sizzled and still he went on building and counting. Finally, he could go on no more. He had spied a lovely green pond in the distance. As he climbed down his long ladder, he counted ninety steps

of the ladder. As soon as he reached the bottom, he ran off and dived into the cool water. In the distance, all that could be seen was his Panama hat bobbing up and down.

Much refreshed, Ponti returned to his bricks. Working, humming and singing, he added and added more bricks to his brick wall. He worked so hard that it was soon night time. Now he worked in the light of the moon and the stars. Now and again, he stopped and looked up. The stars twinkled and winked with encouragement. They seemed so near that Ponti wanted to reach up and touch them. If only he had a longer ladder!

Introduce the digits **1** to **9** in the units together with the digit **2** in the tens columns to make the numbers **21** to **29**.

1. **Read out the following numbers:**

    21, 22, 23, 24, 25, 26, 27, 28, 29

    11, 12, 13, 14, 15, 16, 17, 18, 19, 20

    3, 13, 23, 1, 11, 21, 5, 15, 25, 9, 19, 29

    1, 10, 20, 30, 40, 15, 50, 16, 60, 17, 70

    3, 30, 4, 40, 5, 50, 6, 60, 7, 70, 8, 80, 9, 90

2. **Listen to these numbers and write them down as numerals:**

    Five, twenty, four, thirteen, nineteen, twenty-eight, eight, nought, forty, twenty-one, ten, thirty, seventeen, seventy, eighteen, eighty, nineteen, ninety

3. **Which number is 1 more than 3?**

4. **Which number is 2 more than 28?**

5. **Which number is 1 more than 29?**

6. **Which number is 1 more than 20?**

7. **Which number is 2 more than 20?**

8. **Which number is 3 more than 20?**

9. **Which number is 7 more than 20?**

10. **Which number is 10 more than 10?**

11. **Write down the following sums and write down the answer carefully so that each numeral is clearly in the correct column:**

a.
$$\begin{array}{r} 11 \\ + 15 \\ \hline \\ \hline \end{array}$$

b.
$$\begin{array}{r} 6 \\ + 20 \\ \hline \\ \hline \end{array}$$

c.
$$\begin{array}{r} 19 \\ + 10 \\ \hline \\ \hline \end{array}$$

d.
$$\begin{array}{r} 1 \\ + 20 \\ \hline \\ \hline \end{array}$$

e.
$$\begin{array}{r} 70 \\ + 20 \\ \hline \\ \hline \end{array}$$

f.
$$\begin{array}{r} 9 \\ + 20 \\ \hline \\ \hline \end{array}$$

g.   11
     + 10
     _____

h.   5
      + 20
      _____

i.   15
     + 10
     _____

j.   5
      + 11
      _____

12. Write down the following sums in columns and work out the correct answers:

a. 18 + 21 =

b. 13 + 14 =

c. 15 + 14 =

d. 8 + 20 =

e. 21 + 5 =

f. 6 + 22 =

g. 14 + 14 =

h. 8 + 12 =

i. 26 + 3 =

j. 5 + 14 =

✿ LESSON **SEVENTEEN** ✿

Introduce the digits **1** to **9** in both the units and the tens columns to make the numbers **31** to **39**.

1. **Read out the following numbers:**

   31, 32, 33, 34, 35, 36, 37, 38, 39

   21, 22, 23, 24, 25, 26, 27, 28, 29, 30

   37, 17, 27, 38, 7, 15, 35, 39, 30, 10

   0, 30, 20, 10, 31, 11, 16, 36, 6, 21, 40

   3, 30, 33, 13, 31, 21, 29, 39, 0, 10, 32

2. **Listen to these numbers and write them down as numerals:**

   six, thirty-six, sixteen, seven, seventeen, thirty-seven

   twenty-seven, nought, thirty-one, twenty-three, thirty

   eleven, thirty-eight, thirty-one

3. **Which number is 1 more than 33?**

4. **Which number is 2 more than 38?**

5. Which number is 3 more than 13?

6. Which number is 3 more than 30?

7. Which number is 8 more than 30?

8. Which number is 10 more than 20?

9. Which number is 9 more than 30?

10. Which number is 9 more than 10?

11. Write down the following sums and write down the answer carefully so that each numeral is clearly in the correct column:

a. $\begin{array}{r} 34 \\ + 4 \\ \hline \\ \hline \end{array}$

b. $\begin{array}{r} 8 \\ + 31 \\ \hline \\ \hline \end{array}$

c. $\begin{array}{r} 22 \\ + 13 \\ \hline \\ \hline \end{array}$

d. $\begin{array}{r} 40 \\ + 20 \\ \hline \\ \hline \end{array}$

e. $\begin{array}{r} 28 \\ + 11 \\ \hline \\ \hline \end{array}$

f. $\begin{array}{r} 18 \\ + 21 \\ \hline \\ \hline \end{array}$

g.   5
     + 24
    _____

    _____

h.   4
     + 25
    _____

    _____

i.   6
     + 30
    _____

    _____

j.   13
     + 13
    _____

    _____

12. Write down the following sums in columns and work out the correct answers.

a. **18 + 31 =**

b. **23 + 10 =**

c. **36 + 2 =**

d. **7 + 12 =**

e. **14 + 3 =**

f. **25 + 12 =**

g. **11 + 27 =**

h. **6 + 13 =**

i. **21 + 6 =**

j. **19 + 20 =**

13. Now do these:

a. Ringo runs around the garden path 20 times while he chases a bright yellow ball. He runs around the garden path another 20 times and then has a rest. How many times has he run around the garden path altogether?

b. Ponti counts 15 sweeties in the jar. He adds 20 more. How many sweeties are there now in the jar?

c. Aunty Meg buys 20 balloons for a party. She then remembers that Polly asked for 26 balloons. How many more balloons does she have to buy for Polly?

d. Buttons is a very jolly puppy. He loves doggie biscuits. Yesterday he ate 4 doggie biscuits. Today he was given 6 more for being such an obedient dog. Did he get more doggie biscuits today or yesterday? How many more?

e. There are 70 children in the hall. Another 20 children enter. How many children are there altogether in the hall?

f. 22 boys went to play football. 33 boys went to play cricket. How many boys went to the field to play football and cricket?

g. 8 teddy bears sat on Priti's bed. Her sister bought her 9 more. But they do not fit on the bed, so Priti put them on a sofa. How many teddy bears are now sitting on the sofa?

h. There are 10 little boys in the paddling pool. 10 more join them. How many little boys are now paddling in the pool?

i. An elephant has 1 trunk and 4 legs. Jodi sees 5 elephants. How many trunks and how many legs do all the elephants have?

j.   There are 30 cars in the car park. 3 more cars arrive. 10 minutes later another 5 cars enter the car park. How many cars are there now in the car park?

❧ LESSON **EIGHTEEN** ❧

Introduce the digits **1** to **9** in both the units and the tens columns to make the numbers **41** to **59**.

1. **Read out the following numbers:**

    41, 42, 43, 44, 45, 46, 47, 48, 49

    51, 52, 53, 54, 55, 56, 57, 58, 59

    31, 32, 33, 34, 35, 36, 37, 38, 39, 40

    47, 17, 47, 48, 58, 15, 45, 49, 40, 59

    0, 40, 30, 20, 10, 51, 26, 46, 56, 31, 50

    4, 58, 43, 14, 11, 31, 39, 49, 30, 20, 52

2. **Listen to these numbers and write them down as numerals:**

    thirty, forty-three, thirty-three, fifty-three, forty-one, fifteen

    fifty, fourteen, forty, forty-four, six, sixty, sixteen, forty-six

    nought, ninety, forty-nine, nineteen, forty-nine, thirty-nine

fifty-nine, nineteen, seventy, nought, eighty, fifty-eight

3. **Do these:**

   a. **Write down 1 less than 50.**

   b. **Write down the number that is 3 less than 43.**

   c. **Rita walks on the seashore and counts 30 pebbles. She then counts 20 more pebbles. How many pebbles has she counted altogether?**

   d. **Ron sees some bicycles. He counts up to 31 bicycles and then sees 8 more. How many bicycles has he seen altogether?**

   e. **There are 50 mobile phones in the shop window. Pete sees 9 more in another shop window. How many mobile phones does Pete see altogether?**

   f. **Lots of sheep are standing in the**

warm sunshine. Arabella counts 43 sheep. She looks in another direction and counts another 10 sheep. How many sheep has Arabella counted altogether?

g. Tessa bought a packet of 30 seeds and another packet of 24 seeds. How many seeds did she buy altogether?

h. Write the following numbers in columns and write down the answer: 8 + 41

i. Write down two ways of adding numbers to make 50.

j. Write down 3 ways of adding numbers to make 55.

4. Do these:

a. Which number is 1 more than 33?

b. Which number is 2 more than 38?

c. Which number is 3 more than 30?

d. Which number is 3 more than 13?

e.   Which number is 8 more than 30?

f.   Which number is 10 more than 20?

g.   Which number is 9 more than 30?

h.   Which number is 10 more than 80?

i.   Which number is 7 more than 50?

j.   Which number is 5 more than 50?

5.   Write down the following sums and write down the answer carefully so that each numeral is clearly in the correct column:

a.
$$41$$
$$+\ 14$$
_____
_____

b.
$$32$$
$$+\ 25$$
_____
_____

c.
$$17$$
$$+\ 40$$
_____
_____

d.
$$5$$
$$+\ 53$$
_____
_____

e.
$$50$$
$$+\ 9$$
_____
_____

f.
$$20$$
$$+\ 20$$
_____
_____

g.   30
    + 14
    ———
    ———

h.   8
    + 21
    ———
    ———

i.   19
    + 40
    ———
    ———

j.   18
    + 31
    ———
    ———

6. **Write down the following sums in columns and work out the correct answers.**

   a. **41 + 15 =**

   b. **10 + 49 =**

   c. **14 + 24 =**

   d. **33 + 22 =**

   e. **13 + 32 =**

   f. **42 + 14 =**

   g. **6 + 51 =**

   h. **31 + 21 =**

   i. **18 + 41 =**

   j. **6 + 22 =**

❧ LESSON **NINETEEN** ❧

Introduce the digits **1** to **9** in the units column and the digits **6** to **9** in the tens column to make the numbers **61** to **99**.

1. Read out the following numbers:

61, 62, 63, 64, 65, 66, 67, 68, 69

71, 72, 73, 74, 75, 76, 77, 78, 79

81, 82, 83, 84, 85, 86, 87, 88, 89

91, 92, 93, 94, 95, 96, 97, 98, 99

2. Listen to these numbers and write them down as numerals:

ninety, sixty-nine, seventeen, seventy-one, eight, eighty-three

eighteen, eleven, ninety-nine, fifty-four, sixty-two, six, sixty

ninety-one, thirty-two

3. **Write down the following sums and write down the answer carefully so that each numeral is clearly in the correct column:**

a.
$$33$$
$$+\ 33$$

b.
$$38$$
$$+\ 41$$

c.
$$41$$
$$+\ 28$$

d.
$$60$$
$$+\ 39$$

e.
$$54$$
$$+\ 45$$

f.
$$9$$
$$+\ 90$$

g.
$$6$$
$$+\ 63$$

h.
$$60$$
$$+\ 30$$

i.
$$44$$
$$+\ 55$$

j.
$$51$$
$$+\ 47$$

4. **Write down the following sums in columns and work out the correct answers:**

   a. **6 + 63 =**

   b. **16 + 71 =**

   c. **52 + 42 =**

   d. **81 + 18 =**

   e. **45 + 54 =**

   f. **9 + 90 =**

   g. **19 + 80 =**

   h. **37 + 42 =**

   i. **23 + 43 =**

   j. **80 + 18 =**

5. **Do these:**

   a. **Mandy sees 5 fish swimming in a pond. A little while later she sees another 30 fish swimming in the pond. How many fish has she seen altogether in the pond?**

b. David loves marbles. He has one bag of 17 marbles and another bag of 22 marbles. How many marbles does David have altogether?

c. There are 50 chairs in the hall. Simon brings 9 more chairs into the hall. How many chairs are there now in the hall?

d. On Wednesday, Sandra read 43 pages of her book. The next day she read another 10 pages. How many pages has she read altogether?

e. Tom loves jelly beans. He ate 30 jelly beans in the morning and 28 jelly beans in the afternoon. How many jelly beans did he eat altogether that day?

f. Joanna and her friend decided to count stars in the sky one night. Joanna counted 60 stars and her friend counted another 36 stars. How many stars have they seen altogether?

g. Adam packs 72 ping-pong balls into his sports bag. He finds another 22 ping-pong balls and adds them to his sports bag as well. How many ping-pong balls does he have in his sports bag altogether?

h. Dad's telephone rings 35 times before lunch and 63 times after lunch. How many times does his phone ring that day altogether?

i. Donna collects stickers. She has 44 stickers on one page and 32 stickers on the next page. Her best friend gives her 20 new stickers to add to her collection. How many stickers does Donna now have altogether?

j. Can you think of 5 different ways to make 71 by adding 2 numbers together? Write them down.

❧ LESSON **TWENTY** ❧

Revise the number **10**, which is denoted by one set of ten written as **1** in the tens column and no sets of units written as **0** in the units column (see Lesson Nine).

Similarly, the whole number **100** is denoted by one set of hundreds written as **1** in the hundreds column, no sets of tens written as **0** in the tens column and no sets of units written as **0** in the units column.

Note: the more advanced child may grasp the range of numbers that become available simply by combining the digits **1** to **9** in the units, tens and hundreds columns.

1. **Read out the following numbers:**

    91, 92, 93, 94, 95, 96, 97, 98, 99, 100

    71, 81, 91, 21, 12, 13, 44, 54, 65, 76

    47, 97, 73, 18, 10, 100, 90, 59, 30, 100

    0, 20, 50, 100, 77, 11, 17, 19, 90, 100, 40

    100, 99, 98, 97, 96, 95, 94, 93, 92, 91, 0

2. **Listen to these numbers and write them down as numerals:**

    nought, ten, twelve, twenty, seven, seventeen, one hundred

five, fifty-five, ninety-nine, nineteen, nine, one, eleven, ten

3. **Which number is 1 more than 99?**

4. **Which number is 2 more than 98?**

5. **Which number is 3 more than 97?**

6. **Which number is 4 more than 96?**

7. **Which number is 5 more than 95?**

8. **Which number is 6 more than 94?**

9. **Which number is 7 more than 93?**

10. **Which number is 8 more than 92?**

11. **Which number is 9 more than 91?**

12. **Which number is 10 more than 90?**

13. **Write down the following sums and write down the answer carefully so that each numeral is clearly in the correct column:**

   a. $\begin{array}{r} 11 \\ + 86 \\ \hline \\ \hline \end{array}$
   b. $\begin{array}{r} 45 \\ + 100 \\ \hline \\ \hline \end{array}$

c.
$$6 + 100$$

d.
$$44 + 55$$

e.
$$100 + 0$$

f.
$$10 + 85$$

g.
$$8 + 81$$

h.
$$100 + 90$$

i.
$$100 + 90$$

j.
$$141 + 21$$

14. Write down the following sums in columns and work out the correct answers:

a. **40 + 4 =**

b. **86 + 13 =**

c. **8 + 80 + 1 =**

d. **90 + 0 + 9 =**

e.   **52 + 25 =**

f.   **100 + 91 =**

g.   **900 + 99 =**

h.   **404 + 40 =**

i.   **200 + 300 =**

j.   **444 + 222 =**

15. **Do the following:**

a.   **Candy sees 50 birds in the sky. A little while later she sees another 31 birds in the sky. How many birds has she seen altogether in the sky?**

b.   **Fiona loves sweeties. She has one bag of 70 sweeties and another bag of 27 sweeties. How many sweeties does Fiona have altogether?**

c.   **There are 90 children in the school. If 9 more children join the school, how many children will there then be in the school?**

d. **Jenny loves to read. She has already read 51 books. If she reads another 20 books, how many books will she have read altogether?**

e. **Danny loves pencils. He has 26 pencils in his pencil case. On his birthday, his friends give him 32 new pencils. How many pencils does he now have altogether?**

f. **Julia's father has 41 ties. Her grandfather has 33 ties. How many ties do her father and grandfather have altogether?**

g. **Lucy can see 66 flowers in her garden. She can see another 33 flowers in her neighbour's garden. How many flowers can Lucy see in both gardens?**

h. **Mum's alarm clock rings for 17 seconds every morning and for 12 seconds every evening. For how many seconds does her alarm clock ring each day?**

i.   Sandy collects stamps. She has 11 stamps from France and 41 stamps from Italy. How many stamps does Sandy have from France and Italy altogether?

j.   Can you think of 5 different ways to make 90 by adding 2 numbers together? Write them down.

❧ LESSON **TWENTY-ONE** ❧

It is now appropriate to consider the sequencing of numbers in ascending order. This will aid the child in recognising smaller and larger numbers.

1. **Write down these numbers and draw a circle around the smallest one:**

    a.   **18, 80, 8, 28, 48, 100**

    b.   **40, 14, 15, 25, 24, 50**

    c.   **7, 29, 9, 19, 90, 17, 27**

    d.   **26, 16, 60, 17, 27, 70, 99**

    e.   **30, 29, 100, 17, 27, 19**

2. **Write down these numbers and draw a circle around the largest one:**

    a.   **40, 14, 16, 60, 6, 4**

    b.   **15, 50, 18, 90, 19, 100**

    c.   **30, 40, 50, 16, 70**

    d.   **90, 9, 19, 29, 80, 18**

    e.   **19, 18, 100, 17, 16, 20**

3. **Write down these numbers in the correct order from smallest to largest:**

    a. 18, 20, 17, 16, 19, 21

    b. 90, 30, 50, 60, 80, 70

    c. 6, 9, 7, 10, 5, 4, 3, 90

    d. 25, 30, 28, 19, 13, 100

    e. 29, 20, 40, 13, 3, 10

4. **Write down these numbers in the correct order from largest to smallest:**

    a. 50, 10, 40, 20, 2, 100

    b. 8, 11, 15, 50, 30, 7

    c. 13, 30, 23, 60, 16, 6

    d. 80, 18, 6, 36, 33, 16

    e. 10, 0, 12, 100, 29, 30, 90

5. **Answer these:**

    a. Which number is 10 more than 20?

    b. Which number is 50 more than 10?

c.   Which number is 19 more than 1?

d.   Which number is 9 more than 5?

e.   Which number is 20 less than 40?

f.   Which number is 3 less than 29?

g.   Which number is 7 less than 17?

h.   Which number is 10 less than 30?

i.   Which number is 99 less than 100?

j.   Which number is 1 less than 100?

6.   Now listen to these and answer them aloud:

a.   Mummy has 4 woolly scarves and you have 5 woolly scarves. Who has more? How many more?

b.   4 puppies and 7 cats are playing in the park. Are there more puppies or more cats? How many more?

c.   Annie sang 5 songs and Jenny sang 11 songs at the party. Who sang more songs? How many more?

d. There are 11 pictures hanging on the walls of the classroom and there are 9 pictures hanging in the corridor. Are there more pictures in the classroom or in the corridor? How many more?

e. Today there are 15 children in class. Yesterday there were 21 children in class. Were there more children in class today or yesterday? How many more?

f. Sabrina has 3 goldfish. Her sister has 8 goldfish. Who has fewer goldfish? How many fewer?

g. Oliver sees 3 monkeys and 12 giraffes when he goes to the zoo. Does he see fewer monkeys or giraffes? How many fewer?

h. Patricia writes 3 letters to her brother and 7 letters to her sister. To whom does she write fewer letters? How many fewer?

i.   Frankie puts 5 roses in a blue vase and 8 tulips in a red vase. In which vase does she put fewer flowers? How many fewer?

j.   Fred eats 23 chocolates and Jim eats 6 chocolates more than Fred? How many chocolates does Jim eat?

❧ LESSON **TWENTY-TWO** ❧

Introduce subtraction, denoted by a minus sign (−). Subtraction allows numbers to be decreased by specific amounts; it is the means by which one number is combined with another number to create a lower number. At this stage, subtraction will be restricted to the numbers **1** to **9**.

There are various ways of subtracting numbers:

- **7** 'take away' **3**

- 'Take' **3** 'away from' **7**

- **7** 'minus' **3**

- **7** 'subtract' **3**

- **3** 'less than' **7**.

Note: unlike addition when changing the order of numbers has no effect on the outcome, in subtraction the order of numbers is paramount. Hence, it is particularly important that children do not acquire the bad habit of switching the order of the numbers: **7** take away **3** is not the same as **3** take away **7**.

Once again, children should not add or subtract with the aid of their fingers!

1. Do these:

   a. Take one away from: ten, nine, eight, seven, six, five, four, three, two, one.

   b. Take two away from: ten, nine, eight, seven, six, five, four, three, two.

   c. Take three away from: ten, nine, eight, seven, six, five, four, three.

   d. Take four away from: ten, nine, eight, seven, six, five, four.

   e. Take five away from: ten, nine, eight, seven, six, five.

   f. Take six away from: ten, nine, eight, seven, six.

   g. Take seven away from: ten, nine, eight, seven.

   h. Take eight away from: ten, nine, eight.

   i. Take nine away from: ten, nine.

j. Take ten away from ten.

k. Subtract two from six.

l. Subtract five from nine.

m. Subtract nine from nine.

n. Subtract one from ten.

o. Subtract one from one.

p. What is one less than eight?

q. What is three less than six?

r. What is six less than eight?

s. What is four less than four?

t. What is two less than ten?

2. Write down the signs for addition, subtraction and equals.

3. Write down these sums and work out the correct answers:

a. $6 - 4 =$

b. $8 - 3 =$

c. $9 - 1 =$

d. $6 - 0 =$

e. $4 - 3 =$

f. $1 - 1 =$

g. $7 - 7 =$

h. $2 - 1 =$

i. $1 - 1 =$

j. $5 - 2 =$

4. **Now listen to these and answer them aloud:**

   a. **Kate sees 4 chocolate biscuits on the table. She eats 3 of them. How many are left?**

   b. **Annie loves fruit. There are 10 cherries in the bowl. She eats 5 of them. How many cherries remain in the bowl?**

   c. **Tim sees 8 birds on the grass. 5 birds fly away. How many birds are left on the grass?**

d. Max takes 10 pencils to the art room. He gives 4 of them away. How many pencils does he have left?

e. Tessa had 7 rubbers in her bag. She dropped 4 of them and could not find them. How many rubbers does she now have in her bag?

f. 10 benches stand in the hall. 2 benches are taken out of the hall. How many benches are left in the hall?

g. There are 5 people standing by the window. 3 people leave. How many are left?

h. Dan loves crisps. He buys 4 packets of crisps and eats 2 of the packets. How many packets of crisps does Dan have left?

i. Molly counts 8 oranges. She eats 1 orange. How many oranges are left?

j. Moggy has 8 kittens. 3 kittens are given away. How many kittens does Moggy have left?

5. **Now do these:**

a. I have 7 pencils. If I give 3 pencils to my best friend, how many do I have left?

b. I have 9 pencils. If my best friend gives me 4 more pencils, how many pencils do I have altogether?

c. Priti has 10 pencils. If she gives 7 pencils to Priya, how many pencils will Priti have left?

d. Mum buys 9 potatoes. If 5 of them are bad, how many potatoes are good?

e. Freddie has 10 toys. If he breaks 3 of them, how many will he have left?

f. Zak reads 1 page of his new book. Then he reads 9 more pages. How many pages has Zak read altogether?

g. Leo draws 7 cars. If he rubs 2 of them out, how many cars are left in his book?

h. Angelina puts 9 ribbons in her hair. Her mother says that there are too many ribbons in her hair and tells Angelina to take 5 of the ribbons away. How many ribbons remain in Angelina's hair?

i. John has 9 jelly beans. He gives 3 jelly beans to Peter and 4 jelly beans to Adam. How many jelly beans does John have left?

j. Fred has 10 chocolates. He gives 4 of his friends 1 chocolate each. How many chocolates does Fred have left?

PONTI PANDA CLEANS HIS PLATE

It was a lovely summer evening. The air was fresh, the birds were still chirping and the sky was bright and blue. The songs of at least six different birds could be heard even though they were well hidden in the many trees that stood at the end of the garden. Ponti Panda was satisfied with himself, especially as he could now count further than the fingers on his hands. In fact, he could count from one to a hundred. He could make numbers up and make them equal twenty, thirty, forty, fifty, all the way up to a hundred. If he saw a line of numbers, he could pick out the largest and the smallest. He loved adding numbers because then they got bigger. He liked to eat more chocolate, more cake, more slices of buttered toast. He spent hours and hours counting the grapes on bunches of grapes and counting red cherries in the fruit bowl.

He loved to eat and always left a clean plate at the end of his meal. Since he could count, he always knew how much he had eaten and how much there was left to eat. When he was given five sausages to eat, he knew that after he had eaten three of them there would still be two sausages left for him to eat. If he had a bowl of twenty ripe red cherries, he could eat five cherries and see that he had fifteen left, which meant that he had taken five away. He wondered whether there was a special word for taking things away. He turned over the next page of his arithmetic book and saw a long new word. It was subtraction, the opposite of addition. Things could be added and they could be subtracted. If you added, you made more; if you subtracted, you made less. You could do this with grapes, with cherries, with chocolates, with all the numbers from one to a hundred. Taking away was a new game to play with numbers.

1. **Do these:**

   a. **Take one away from: twenty, nineteen, eighteen, seventeen, sixteen, fifteen, fourteen, thirteen, twelve, eleven.**

   b. **Take two away from: twenty, nineteen, eighteen, seventeen, sixteen, fifteen, fourteen, thirteen, twelve.**

   c. **Take three away from: twenty, nineteen, eighteen, seventeen, sixteen, fifteen, fourteen, thirteen.**

   d. **Take four away from: twenty, nineteen, eighteen, seventeen, sixteen, fifteen, fourteen.**

   e. **Take five away from: twenty, nineteen, eighteen, seventeen, sixteen, fifteen.**

f.   Take six away from: twenty, nineteen, eighteen, seventeen, sixteen.

g.   Take seven away from: twenty, nineteen, eighteen, seventeen.

h.   Take eight away from: twenty, nineteen, eighteen.

i.   Take nine away from: twenty, nineteen.

j.   Take ten away from twenty.

2.   **Now do these:**

a.   Subtract 2 from 20.

b.   Subtract 4 from 14.

c.   Subtract 5 from 19.

d.   Subtract 11 from 15.

e.   Subtract 10 from 20.

f.   Take 3 away from 13.

g.   Take 8 away from 10.

h.   **What is 6 less than 16?**

i.   **What is 1 less than 17?**

j.   **What is 5 minus 4?**

k.   **What is 20 minus 10?**

l.   **What is 19 minus 9?**

3. **Write down these sums and work out the correct answers:**

a.   **20 − 10 =**

b.   **15 − 5 =**

c.   **13 − 2 =**

d.   **19 − 7 =**

e.   **16 − 10 =**

f.   **11 − 1 =**

g.   **17 − 5 =**

h.   **20 − 20 =**

i.   **9 − 6 =**

j.   **18 − 7 =**

4. Write down the following sums and write down the answer carefully so that each numeral is clearly in the correct column:

a.
$$\begin{array}{r} 20 \\ -\ 10 \\ \hline \\ \hline \end{array}$$

b.
$$\begin{array}{r} 19 \\ -\ 10 \\ \hline \\ \hline \end{array}$$

c.
$$\begin{array}{r} 16 \\ -3 \\ \hline \\ \hline \end{array}$$

d.
$$\begin{array}{r} 13 \\ -2 \\ \hline \\ \hline \end{array}$$

e.
$$\begin{array}{r} 11 \\ -10 \\ \hline \\ \hline \end{array}$$

f.
$$\begin{array}{r} 15 \\ -5 \\ \hline \\ \hline \end{array}$$

g.
$$\begin{array}{r} 18 \\ -\ 16 \\ \hline \\ \hline \end{array}$$

h.
$$\begin{array}{r} 17 \\ -13 \\ \hline \\ \hline \end{array}$$

i.
$$\begin{array}{r} 14 \\ -4 \\ \hline \\ \hline \end{array}$$

j.
$$\begin{array}{r} 12 \\ -2 \\ \hline \\ \hline \end{array}$$

Note: in the case of those children who are not yet proficient readers, the following problems should be read aloud to facilitate comprehension.

5. **Do these:**

   a. **There are 19 biscuits in the biscuit tin. Fran eats 3 biscuits and Toby eats another 4 biscuits. How many biscuits are left in the tin?**

   b. **There are 20 books on the teacher's desk. The teacher gives out 10 books. How many books are left on her desk?**

   c. **There are 16 paint brushes in the tin. Peter takes 4 brushes out of the tin. How many paint brushes are left in the tin?**

   d. **18 horses gallop over the fence. 7 of them turn left and the rest turn right. How many horses turned right?**

   e. **There are 20 sheets of paper on the desk. If you use 6 sheets of paper, how many are left?**

f.   Jill goes shopping. She has £17 to spend. If she only spends £5, how much money will she have left?

g.   Today, 5 children are absent from the class. Usually, there are 19 children in the class. How many children are in class today?

h.   Tina draws 16 straight lines on one page of her book. On the next page, she draws 23 lines. How many lines has she drawn altogether?

i.   Sophie likes to draw teddy bears. She draws 24 teddy bears and then draws another 24. How many teddy bears has Sophie drawn altogether?

j.   Dave is baking a big birthday cake. He has 18 eggs. He uses 6 eggs for the sponge and 4 eggs for the filling. How many eggs does he have left?

❧ LESSON **TWENTY-FOUR** ❧

Introduce subtraction of numbers with digits **1** to **9** in the tens column and **0** in the units column: **30**, **40**, **50**, **60**, **70**, **80**, **90**. Revise (as set out in Lesson Twenty-Two) the various ways of referring to subtraction.

1. Do these:

a. Take ten away from: ten, twenty, thirty, forty, fifty, sixty, seventy, eighty, ninety.

b. Take twenty away from: twenty, thirty, forty, fifty, sixty, seventy, eighty, ninety.

c. Take thirty away from: thirty, forty, fifty, sixty, seventy, eighty, ninety.

d. Take forty away from: forty, fifty, sixty, seventy, eighty, ninety.

e. Take fifty away from: fifty, sixty, seventy, eighty, ninety.

f. Take sixty away from: sixty, seventy, eighty, ninety.

g. Take seventy away from: seventy, eighty, ninety.

h. Take eighty away from: eighty, ninety.

i. Take ninety away from ninety.

2. **Now do these:**

a. Subtract 10 from 20.

b. Take 10 away from 90.

c. 80 minus 20.

d. What is 30 less than 70?

e. Take 50 away from 90.

f. Subtract 40 from 60.

g. 50 minus 30.

h. Subtract 70 from 80.

i. What is 60 less than 90?

j. Subtract 10 from 10.

3. **Write down these sums and work out the correct answers:**

    a. **40 − 10 =**

    b. **50 − 20 =**

    c. **30 − 10 =**

    d. **90 − 20 =**

    e. **20 − 10 =**

    f. **80 − 40 =**

    g. **60 − 20 =**

    h. **16 − 6 =**

    i. **17 − 4 =**

    j. **19 − 8 =**

4. **Write down the following sums and write down the answer carefully so that each numeral is placed clearly in the correct column:**

a.
$$\begin{array}{r} 80 \\ -10 \\ \hline \\ \hline \end{array}$$

b.
$$\begin{array}{r} 40 \\ -30 \\ \hline \\ \hline \end{array}$$

c.
$$\begin{array}{r} 50 \\ -40 \\ \hline \\ \hline \end{array}$$

d.
$$\begin{array}{r} 66 \\ -56 \\ \hline \\ \hline \end{array}$$

e.
$$\begin{array}{r} 83 \\ -62 \\ \hline \\ \hline \end{array}$$

f.
$$\begin{array}{r} 75 \\ -14 \\ \hline \\ \hline \end{array}$$

g.
$$\begin{array}{r} 99 \\ -8 \\ \hline \\ \hline \end{array}$$

h.
$$\begin{array}{r} 38 \\ -15 \\ \hline \\ \hline \end{array}$$

i.
$$\begin{array}{r} 19 \\ -8 \\ \hline \\ \hline \end{array}$$

j.
$$\begin{array}{r} 69 \\ -44 \\ \hline \\ \hline \end{array}$$

Note: in the case of those children who are not yet proficient readers, the following problems should be read aloud to facilitate comprehension.

5. **Do these:**

   a. There are 30 marbles in a box. Bobby takes out 10 marbles and Dara takes out 15 marbles. How many marbles are left in the box?

   b. There are 50 postcards on the wall. The teacher takes down 20 postcards. How many postcards are left on the wall?

   c. Yesterday, 20 children went on an outing. If there are 90 children in the school, how many children did not go on the outing?

   d. Toni goes shopping. She has 80 pence in her purse. She spends 30 pence at the shop. How many pence does she now have left in her purse?

   e. Josie is baking cookies for her

party. She bakes 30 cookies and her little brother eats 10 of them straightaway. How many cookies does she have left for her party?

f. Sabrina likes to make paper flowers. She makes 60 flowers and takes 20 of them to school to give to her friends. How many flowers does she now have left?

g. Grandpa loves to write letters. Last month he wrote 50 letters to his friends. He did not have enough stamps so he could only send 30 letters. How many more stamps will he need to buy so that he can send all his letters?

h. There are 10 pictures in the classroom and there are 30 pictures in the Art Room. How many fewer pictures are there in the classroom than in the Art Room? How many pictures are there altogether in the classroom and the Art Room?

i. **Tonga has 10 pairs of shoes. Her sister has 20 pairs of shoes. How many fewer pairs of shoes does Tonga have than her sister? How many pairs of shoes do they have altogether?**

j. **Max sings 12 songs at the Christmas concert. His best friend, Sam, sings 6 songs. How many more songs does Max sing than Sam? How many fewer songs does Sam sing than Max?**

❧ LESSON **TWENTY-FIVE** ❧

Introduce subtraction of numbers with digits **1** to **9** in the tens column and in the units column so that all numbers, **1** to **99**, can be used in subtraction sums 'without borrowing'. Obviously, it is not possible to subtract from **100** 'without borrowing'.

1. Write down the following sums and work out the correct answers:

a.
$$\begin{array}{r} 42 \\ -\ 11 \\ \hline \\ \hline \end{array}$$

b.
$$\begin{array}{r} 86 \\ -34 \\ \hline \\ \hline \end{array}$$

c.
$$\begin{array}{r} 79 \\ -38 \\ \hline \\ \hline \end{array}$$

d.
$$\begin{array}{r} 43 \\ -23 \\ \hline \\ \hline \end{array}$$

e.
$$\begin{array}{r} 72 \\ -50 \\ \hline \\ \hline \end{array}$$

f.
$$\begin{array}{r} 68 \\ -54 \\ \hline \\ \hline \end{array}$$

g.
$$\begin{array}{r} 97 \\ -76 \\ \hline \\ \hline \end{array}$$

h.
$$\begin{array}{r} 55 \\ -4 \\ \hline \\ \hline \end{array}$$

i.
$$67$$
$$-3$$
_____

j.
$$99$$
$$-9$$
_____

2. **Write down the following sums and work out the correct answers:**

a. **32 − 21 =**

b. **89 − 44 =**

c. **48 − 6 =**

d. **99 − 10 =**

e. **63 − 60 =**

f. **47 − 16 =**

g. **55 − 22 =**

h. **28 − 18 =**

i. **75 − 23 =**

j. **91 − 11 =**

Note: in the case of those children who are not yet proficient readers, the following problems should be read aloud to facilitate comprehension.

3. **Now do these:**

a. **There are 44 newspapers on the stand. Mr Pinksy buys 12 of them. How many newspapers are left on the stand?**

b. **Len is having a party and his Mum buys 59 balloons. 15 of them are put in the hall and the remainder are put in the dining room. How many balloons are in the dining room?**

c. **Write down five different ways of making the number 5 by subtracting one number from another number.**

d. **Choose two of the following numbers to add together to give 20: 6, 13, 12, 14, 19**

e. **Write down five different ways of making the number 20 by subtracting one number from another number.**

f. Max loves to play with toy animals. He has 24 elephants and 13 monkeys. How many fewer monkeys does he have than elephants? How many toy animals does he have altogether?

g. Meg goes shopping. She has 99 pence in her pocket. After she has spent 54 pence, how much money will she have left in her pocket?

h. Tilly has 26 biscuits in a jar. If she removes 14 biscuits for a tea party, how many biscuits will she have left in the jar?

i. There are 58 fish in the aquarium. The owner of the pet shop sells 37 fish. How many fish still remain in the aquarium?

j. There are 85 packets of crisps on the counter. Tom picks up 12 packets of crisps. How many packets of crisps will be left? Tara picks up another 3 packets of crisps.

How many packets of crisps are now left on the counter?

k. **Beth draws 19 circles on a sheet of paper. She rubs out 5 of them because they are too big. How many circles remain on the sheet of paper?**

❧ LESSON **TWENTY-SIX** ❧

Revise addition and subtraction, 'without carrying' and 'without borrowing'.

Note: it is essential that children set out their work so that numerals are clearly written down in the correct columns; numerals must not straddle two columns.

1. Write down the following sums and work out the correct answers:

a.
$$\begin{array}{r} 96 \\ -84 \\ \hline \\ \hline \end{array}$$

b.
$$\begin{array}{r} 54 \\ -43 \\ \hline \\ \hline \end{array}$$

c.
$$\begin{array}{r} 92 \\ +6 \\ \hline \\ \hline \end{array}$$

d.
$$\begin{array}{r} 65 \\ +33 \\ \hline \\ \hline \end{array}$$

e.
$$\begin{array}{r} 91 \\ -71 \\ \hline \\ \hline \end{array}$$

f.
$$\begin{array}{r} 66 \\ -33 \\ \hline \\ \hline \end{array}$$

g.
$$\begin{array}{r} 96 \\ -61 \\ \hline \\ \hline \end{array}$$

h.
$$\begin{array}{r} 57 \\ +12 \\ \hline \\ \hline \end{array}$$

i.   13
     +72
    ——

    ——

j.   40
    −20
    ——

    ——

2. **Now write down the following sums and work out the correct answers:**

    a. $46 + 33 =$

    b. $87 - 24 =$

    c. $67 - 17 =$

    d. $28 + 71 =$

    e. $59 - 36 =$

    f. $13 + 44 =$

    g. $49 - 15 =$

    h. $34 + 34 =$

    i. $29 - 7 =$

    j. $91 + 8 =$

3. **Do these:**

    a.   **Which number is 2 less than 82?**

b. **Which number is 8 less than 68?**

c. **Which number is 4 less than 44?**

d. **Which number is 9 less than 19?**

e. **Which number is 3 less than 77?**

f. **Which number is 15 less than 56?**

g. **Which number is 66 less than 98?**

h. **Which number is 38 less than 89?**

i. **Which number is 27 less than 77?**

j. **Which number is 13 less than 39?**

4. **Write down five different ways of making 22 by subtracting one number from another number.**

5. **Choose two of the following numbers to add together to make 43:**

   11, 25, 32, 7, 6, 5, 4

6. **Add the smallest number to the largest number from the following numbers:**

   6, 16, 72, 61, 60

7. **Add the largest number to the smallest number from the following numbers:**

   13, 3, 30, 39, 36, 63

8. **Subtract the smallest number from the largest number from the following numbers:**

   14, 43, 20, 3, 30

9. **Write down the following numbers in order from the smallest to the largest, and then subtract the smallest number from the largest number:**

   48, 19, 52, 16, 26, 69, 63

10. **Pip buys lots of presents for his sister. He buys 7 postcards, 12 stickers and 20 marbles. How many postcards and marbles does he buy for his sister? How many stickers and marbles does he buy for his sister? How many presents does he buy altogether for his sister?**

❧ LESSON **TWENTY-SEVEN** ❧

MENTAL ARITHMETIC

Revision and practice of mental arithmetic with the numbers **1** to **20**, using both addition and subtraction.

The importance of mental arithmetic cannot be overstated. Children must learn to add and subtract numbers, in particular from **1** to **20**, without writing them down and without using physical prompts such as fingers, charts, straws, etc. It is essential that children continue to practise mental arithmetic until they are accustomed to answering at speed, automatically as it were.

This ability to add and subtract numbers from **1** to **20** 'in one's head' should be embedded before the child proceeds to addition 'with carrying' and subtraction sums 'with borrowing' (see Chapters 28 and 29).

The mastery of mental arithmetic facilitates the manipulation of numbers in and out of sequence. It fixes number bonds in the child's mind. When adding two numbers, for example **5** and **4**, it is counter-productive to go through every number from **1** to **9** or even from **6** to **9**, in steps of one as it were. The two numbers, **5** and **4**, should be added in one step to make **9**. Otherwise, one is naming numbers in sequence which serves a different purpose to addition or subtraction.

The exercises below can, and should, be used repeatedly in different variations, with the numbers in a different order.

1. **Practise the following addition sums 'in one step' and at speed:**

   $5 + 5$ $6 + 3$ $3 + 3$ $2 + 7$ $2 + 5$
   $4 + 4$ $3 + 5$ $1 + 7$ $2 + 8$ $1 + 9$

2. **Practise the following subtraction sums 'in one step' and at speed:**

   $6 - 2$ $5 - 4$ $9 - 3$ $7 - 4$ $8 - 8$
   $9 - 4$ $9 - 5$ $4 - 3$ $8 - 5$ $10 - 4$

3. **Practise the following addition and subtraction sums 'in one step' and at speed:**

   $6 + 3$ $10 - 6$ $6 + 4$ $3 + 7$ $8 - 5$
   $8 - 8$ $9 - 4$ $3 + 7$ $7 - 3$ $5 - 3$

4. **Now practise adding these sums:**

   $10 + 10$ $3 + 10$ $6 + 6$ $5 + 6$
   $7 + 7$ $7 + 10$ $9 + 10$ $3 + 11$

   $3 + 12$ $8 + 7$ $8 + 8$ $9 + 9$
   $5 + 9$ $6 + 8$ $8 + 5$ $5 + 9$

5. **Now practise the following subtraction sums, using the numbers 1 to 20, 'in one step' and at speed:**

    $7 - 7$ $14 - 7$ $7 - 5$ $17 - 5$
    $17 - 15$ $12 - 9$ $19 - 12$ $9 - 2$

    $19 - 16$ $16 - 5$ $15 - 10$ $15 - 9$
    $18 - 10$ $17 - 11$ $15 - 12$

6. **Practise the following addition and subtraction sums, using the numbers 1 to 20, 'in one step' and at speed:**

    $18 - 7$ $13 - 5$ $6 + 9$ $7 + 11$
    $15 - 6$ $14 + 2$ $14 - 6$ $13 + 4$

    $16 - 5$ $20 - 9$ $4 + 9$ $12 - 8$
    $17 - 8$ $16 - 7$ $11 - 4$ $9 + 8$

    $13 + 3$ $20 - 7$ $19 - 8$ $16 + 4$

❧ LESSON **TWENTY-EIGHT** ❧

Introduce addition with 'carrying on' from the units column to the tens column. This enlarges the range of numbers that can be added together.

EXAMPLES:

```
    46              18               9
  +49             +64             +42
  ————            ————            ————
    95              82              51
```
1 (carried over)   1 (carried over)   1 (carried over)

1. Write down the following sums and work out the correct answers, showing clearly the single unit of ten that should be carried over from the units column to the tens column:

a.   **35**
     +5
    ————
    ————

b.   **58**
     +3
    ————
    ————

c.   **25**
     +6
    ————
    ————

d.   **88**
     +6
    ————
    ————

e.
$$\begin{array}{r} 34 \\ +7 \\ \hline \\ \hline \end{array}$$

f.
$$\begin{array}{r} 75 \\ +15 \\ \hline \\ \hline \end{array}$$

g.
$$\begin{array}{r} 33 \\ +7 \\ \hline \\ \hline \end{array}$$

h.
$$\begin{array}{r} 46 \\ +4 \\ \hline \\ \hline \end{array}$$

i.
$$\begin{array}{r} 89 \\ +1 \\ \hline \\ \hline \end{array}$$

j.
$$\begin{array}{r} 63 \\ +36 \\ \hline \\ \hline \end{array}$$

2. **Write down the following sums and give the correct answers, setting each sum out in the correct columns and showing clearly the number carried to the tens column.**

   a. **36 + 48 =**

   b. **54 + 5 =**

   c. **40 + 9 =**

   d. **61 + 9 =**

   e. **54 + 16 =**

f.   75 + 15 =

g.   18 + 80 =

h.   26 + 44 =

i.   93 + 6 =

j.   71 + 9 =

3. **Write down the following numbers in order from the smallest to the largest, and then add the smallest number to the largest number:**

48, 39, 84, 81, 15

46, 6, 64, 16, 41

67, 17, 7, 77, 27

22, 2, 12, 21, 11

13, 31, 3, 33, 23

4. **Write down the following numbers in order from the largest to the smallest, and then add the largest number to the smallest number:**

48, 4, 14, 46, 16, 56

81, 19, 9, 7, 89, 17

55, 15, 17, 57, 75

61, 9, 19, 66, 16

70, 73, 7, 37, 30

5. **Write these down as sums and work out the correct answers:**

Note: writing out the appropriate sums is *not* the same as writing out the question. At the same time, children should now learn that addition may be denoted by different verbal expressions.

a. **What is the total of 16 and 34?**

b. **Add together 73 and 25.**

c. **What is 42 plus 39?**

d. **Add 10 to 89.**

e. **What is the sum of 62 and 29?**

6. Now do these:

Note: those children who are proficient readers should now learn that numbers may be expressed in words or numerals.

a. Lola loves to skip. She skips eight times and then adds another thirty-three skips. How many times does she skip altogether?

b. Zara collects twenty-four conkers and Fran has thirty-six conkers. How many do they have altogether?

c. John has sixteen toy cars, Peter has twenty-five toy cars and James has eleven toy cars. How many toy cars do Peter and James have? How many toy cars do John and James have?

d. There are three books on the desk. One of them has twenty-four pictures. Another has forty-eight pictures. How many pictures are there altogether?

e. Sixteen apples have fallen onto the grass. Ben picks all of them up and adds them to his own basket in which there are already fifteen apples. How many apples does Ben now have in his basket?

f. There are twenty-eight packets of biscuits on one shelf and forty-three packets of biscuits on another shelf. How many packets are there altogether?

g. There are forty-nine sheets of paper in the folder and thirty-three sheets of paper in another folder. How many sheets of paper are there altogether in both folders?

h. There are thirty-three pupils in Year One and twenty-six pupils in Year Two. How many pupils are there altogether?

i. There are twenty-five newspapers on the table and thirty-eight newspapers on the chair. How many newspapers are there altogether?

j. One jar has seventy-three lollies in it. Jenny adds another eighteen lollies to the jar. How many lollies are in the jar now?

❦ LESSON **TWENTY-NINE** ❦

Introduce subtraction with 'borrowing' from the tens column to the units column. This enlarges the range of numbers that can be subtracted from one another.

EXAMPLE:

$$\begin{array}{r} {}^5\cancel{6}{}^14 \\ -38 \\ \hline 26 \\ \hline \end{array}$$

(The **4** in the units column has become **14** thanks to the 'borrowing' of one group of ten from the **6** tens.)

1. **Write down the following sums and work out the correct answers, showing clearly the single unit of ten that has been 'borrowed' from the tens column to be added to the units column:**

a. $$\begin{array}{r} 63 \\ -38 \\ \hline \\ \hline \end{array}$$

b. $$\begin{array}{r} 51 \\ -12 \\ \hline \\ \hline \end{array}$$

c. $$\begin{array}{r} 73 \\ -64 \\ \hline \\ \hline \end{array}$$

d. $$\begin{array}{r} 82 \\ -65 \\ \hline \\ \hline \end{array}$$

e. $\begin{array}{r} 90 \\ -18 \\ \hline \\ \hline \end{array}$ f. $\begin{array}{r} 34 \\ -15 \\ \hline \\ \hline \end{array}$

g. $\begin{array}{r} 65 \\ -46 \\ \hline \\ \hline \end{array}$ h. $\begin{array}{r} 46 \\ -18 \\ \hline \\ \hline \end{array}$

i. $\begin{array}{r} 40 \\ -21 \\ \hline \\ \hline \end{array}$ j. $\begin{array}{r} 54 \\ -23 \\ \hline \\ \hline \end{array}$

2. **Write down the following sums and give the correct answers, setting each sum out in the correct columns and showing clearly the number 'borrowed' from the tens column to be transferred to the units column:**

   a. **29 – 18 =**

   b. **31 – 19 =**

   c. **55 – 38 =**

   d. **61 – 33 =**

e. **80 − 18 =**

f. **74 − 27 =**

g. **38 − 18 =**

h. **99 − 80 =**

i. **63 − 38 =**

j. **72 − 27 =**

3. **Write down the following numbers in order from the smallest to the largest, and then subtract the smallest number from the largest number:**

63, 39, 29, 36, 77

18, 83, 55, 82, 28

46, 37, 95, 48, 38

87, 29, 34, 43, 68

19, 9, 91, 11, 10

4. **Write these down as sums and work out the correct answers:**

    a. **Subtract 41 from 89.**

    b. **Take 39 away from 98.**

    c. **What is 66 minus 39?**

    d. **What is 74 minus 47?**

    e. **Take 23 away from 42.**

5. **Now do these:**

Note: in the case of those children who are not yet proficient readers, the following problems should be read aloud to facilitate comprehension. Those who are proficient readers should once again be reminded that numbers may be expressed in numerals or in words.

    a. **Sammy has twenty-four marbles. He gives nineteen of them to his best friend. How many marbles does Sammy have left?**

    b. **Lola sees thirteen chocolates in a box. She takes out six chocolates and eats them up. How many chocolates remain in the box?**

c. Priti cooks forty little cakes for her friends. They eat thirty-three of them. How many little cakes are left?

d. If Ben uses up twenty-nine sheets of paper for his drawings and there were fifty sheets of paper to begin with, how many sheets of paper are left?

e. There were eighty apples in the box. Sixty-four apples were sold. How many apples remained in the box?

f. There are eighty straws in a packet. If the children use fifty-eight straws, how many straws will remain in the packet?

g. My dog loves chocolate drops. If I give him twelve chocolate drops out of my packet of twenty-one, how many chocolate drops will be left in my packet?

h. There are fifty boxes of biscuits on

the supermarket shelf. If nineteen boxes are sold, how many boxes of biscuits will remain?

i.   There were eighty-six cars in the car park at the beginning of the day. By lunch time, forty-eight cars had gone. How many cars were left in the car park?

j.   If Mrs Fizz sold fifty-six bottles of lemonade at the school fete and she had eighty-two bottles of lemonade to begin with, how many bottles of lemonade remained?

Revise addition with 'carrying' and subtraction with 'borrowing' of two-digit numbers.

1. **Write down the following sums and give the correct answers, showing the working-out clearly:**

a.
$$41$$
$$-\ 26$$
$$\overline{}$$

b.
$$71$$
$$+19$$
$$\overline{}$$

c.
$$64$$
$$+26$$
$$\overline{}$$

d.
$$81$$
$$-54$$
$$\overline{}$$

e.
$$19$$
$$+19$$
$$\overline{}$$

f.
$$28$$
$$-11$$
$$\overline{}$$

g.
$$54$$
$$-18$$
$$\overline{}$$

h.
$$93$$
$$-17$$
$$\overline{}$$

i. $\begin{array}{r} 62 \\ +25 \\ \hline \\ \hline \end{array}$

j. $\begin{array}{r} 49 \\ +38 \\ \hline \\ \hline \end{array}$

2. **Write down the following sums and give the correct answers, showing the working-out clearly:**

   a. **Fran has 22 pencils. If she gives 8 pencils to her best friend, how many does she have left?**

   b. **Huck has 18 pens. If his best friend gives him 23 new pens, how many pens does Huck have now?**

   c. **Anna collects stickers. She has 26 stickers and her little sister gives her 25 more stickers. How many stickers does Anna have now?**

   d. **Lori has 29 books. If her granny gives her 21 new books, how many books will Lori have then?**

   e. **Andy's mother buys 92 potatoes. If she loses 26 potatoes, how many potatoes will she have left?**

f.   Rico has 15 toy cars. If he gives 6 of them to his brother, how many toy cars will Rico have then?

g.   Waylon has 14 rabbits. 5 of them run away. How many rabbits does Waylon have left?

h.   Miss Flossy has 19 pupils. 28 new pupils arrive. How many pupils does Miss Flossy have altogether?

i.   Belinda has 28 fluffy teddy bears. She is given 26 more. How many fluffy teddy bears does Belinda have now?

j.   Ziggy loves collecting shells. He has 84 in his plastic bucket. Then he finds another 18 shells which he adds to his bucket. How many shells does Ziggy have now in his plastic bucket?

3.   Write down five different ways of adding two numbers to give 90.

4. **Write down five different ways of making the number 21 by subtracting one number from another number.**

5. **Choose two of the following numbers to add together to make 89:**

   42, 62, 19, 18, 17, 72, 82

6. **From the following numbers, subtract one number from another to make 29:**

   50, 40, 30, 11, 12, 13

❦ LESSON **THIRTY-ONE** ❦

Introduce subtraction from 100. The principle of 'borrowing' from the tens column may be extended to 'borrowing' from the hundreds column (see Lesson Twenty-Nine).

EXAMPLE:

$$\begin{array}{r} \cancel{1}^{1}00 \\ -\ 60 \\ \hline 40 \\ \hline \end{array}$$

In order to perform the subtraction, first one borrows from the hundreds column, leaving nothing in the hundreds column and ten lots of ten in the tens column.

1. Write down the following sums and give the correct answers, showing the working-out clearly:

a.
$$\begin{array}{r} 100 \\ -\ 40 \\ \hline \\ \hline \end{array}$$

b.
$$\begin{array}{r} 100 \\ -60 \\ \hline \\ \hline \end{array}$$

c.
$$\begin{array}{r} 100 \\ -50 \\ \hline \\ \hline \end{array}$$

d.
$$\begin{array}{r} 100 \\ -70 \\ \hline \\ \hline \end{array}$$

e.   100
    − 30
    _____

    _____

f.   100
    − 10
    _____

    _____

g.   100
    − 20
    _____

    _____

h.   100
    − 90
    _____

    _____

i.   100
    − 80
    _____

    _____

j.   100
    − 100
    _____

    _____

2. **From the following numbers, subtract one number from the other to make 60:**

    90, 40, 50, 20, 70, 100

3. **From the following numbers, subtract one number from the other to make 30:**

    50, 10, 70, 90, 100, 30

❦ LESSON **THIRTY-TWO** ❦

Introduce subtraction in which the principle of 'borrowing' is further extended to 'borrowing' from both the tens and the hundreds column in the same sum.

EXAMPLE:

$$\begin{array}{r} 1^9\theta^10 \\ -6\,4 \\ \hline 3\,6 \\ \hline \end{array}$$

(First one borrows from the hundreds column, leaving nothing in the hundreds column and ten lots of ten in the tens column; then one borrows one lot of the ten lots of ten from the tens column, leaving nine lots of ten in the tens column and ten units in the units column.)

1. Write down the following sums and give the correct answers, showing the working-out clearly:

a.
$$\begin{array}{r} 100 \\ -41 \\ \hline \\ \hline \end{array}$$

b.
$$\begin{array}{r} 100 \\ -62 \\ \hline \\ \hline \end{array}$$

c.
$$\begin{array}{r} 100 \\ -55 \\ \hline \\ \hline \end{array}$$

d.
$$\begin{array}{r} 100 \\ -77 \\ \hline \\ \hline \end{array}$$

e. $\begin{array}{r} 100 \\ -39 \\ \hline \\ \hline \end{array}$ f. $\begin{array}{r} 100 \\ -12 \\ \hline \\ \hline \end{array}$

g. $\begin{array}{r} 100 \\ -26 \\ \hline \\ \hline \end{array}$ h. $\begin{array}{r} 100 \\ -99 \\ \hline \\ \hline \end{array}$

i. $\begin{array}{r} 100 \\ -88 \\ \hline \\ \hline \end{array}$ j. $\begin{array}{r} 100 \\ -3 \\ \hline \\ \hline \end{array}$

2. **From the following numbers, subtract one number from the other to make 64:**

   92, 44, 50, 28, 94, 100

3. **From the following numbers, subtract one number from the other to make 39:**

   56, 18, 77, 99, 100, 57

❦ LESSON **THIRTY-THREE** ❦

Introduce three-digit numbers from **101** to **999**. Practise adding three-digit numbers 'without carrying'.

EXAMPLE:

$$\begin{array}{r} 404 \\ +145 \\ \hline 549 \\ \hline \end{array}$$

At this stage it may be appropriate to show the more advanced child just how extensively the use of columns may be applied:

- **1** in the units column has the value of one.

- **1** in the tens column has the value of ten.

- **1** in the hundreds column has the value of one hundred.

- **1** in the thousands column has the value of one thousand.

- **1** in the ten thousands column has the value of ten thousand.

- **1** in the hundred thousands column has the value of one hundred thousand.

In the number **111,111** (one hundred and eleven thousand, one hundred and eleven), the same numeral has a different value because of the column in which it appears.

1. **Read out the following numbers:**

    186, 420, 632, 938, 98, 101

    9, 909, 99, 990, 999, 919

    67, 607, 706, 76, 670, 760

    303, 33, 333, 300, 30, 330

    40, 440, 44, 405, 550, 445

2. **Now listen to the these numbers and write them down carefully:**

    *   **Two hundred and twenty-two**

    *   **Five hundred and fifty**

    *   **Thirty-five**

    *   **Three hundred and five**

    *   **Six hundred and sixty-five**

    *   **Seventy**

    *   **Seven hundred and seven**

    *   **One hundred and one**

    *   **One hundred and ten**

- **Nine hundred and ninety-one**

- **Ninety**

- **Two hundred and nineteen**

- **Eighty-six**

- **Six hundred and eighty**

- **Eight hundred and eighteen**

- **Eleven**

- **One hundred and ten**

Note: children with the appropriate level of literacy ought to practise further by transposing numbers in writing to numbers in numerals. The greater the facility of a child to write down such numbers, both by hearing them or by reading them, the better.

3. **Write down the answers to the following questions, without setting them out as sums:**

   a. **Which number is 10 more than 100?**

   b. **Which number is 11 more than 100?**

   c. **Which number is 20 more than 100?**

d. Which number is 21 more than 100?

e. Which number is 5 more than 100?

f. Which number is 55 more than 100?

g. Which number is 16 more than 100?

h. Which number is 60 more than 100?

i. Which number is 66 more than 100?

j. Which number is 100 more than 100?

4. **Write down the following sums and give the correct answers, showing the working-out clearly:**

TAKE CARE TO WRITE EACH NUMERAL IN THE CORRECT COLUMN

a.
$$404 + 42$$

b.
$$106 + 160$$

c.
$$203 + 30$$

d.
$$540 + 55$$

e. $\begin{array}{r} 91 \\ +108 \\ \hline \\ \hline \end{array}$ f. $\begin{array}{r} 64 \\ +604 \\ \hline \\ \hline \end{array}$

g. $\begin{array}{r} 800 \\ +100 \\ \hline \\ \hline \end{array}$ h. $\begin{array}{r} 770 \\ +7 \\ \hline \\ \hline \end{array}$

i. $\begin{array}{r} 600 \\ +333 \\ \hline \\ \hline \end{array}$ j. $\begin{array}{r} 48 \\ +401 \\ \hline \\ \hline \end{array}$

5. **Write down the following sums and give the correct answers, setting each sum out in the correct columns:**

   a. **123 + 46 =**

   b. **48 + 40 =**

   c. **800 + 18 =**

   d. **550 + 105 =**

   e. **40 + 404 =**

   f. **3 + 303 =**

g. $606 + 60 =$

h. $19 + 900 =$

i. $700 + 10 =$

j. $59 + 910 =$

6. Write down the following sums and give the correct answers, showing the working-out clearly, with each numeral in the correct column:

a. There are two big books in the library. One has 303 pages and the other has 441 pages. How many pages will the two books have altogether?

b. One sack of potatoes contains 240 potatoes. Another sack contains 312 potatoes. How many potatoes are there altogether in both sacks?

c. There are 120 peanuts in one bag and 330 peanuts in another bag. How many peanuts are there altogether in both bags?

d. There are 25 chickens in the shed. Another 44 chickens join them. How many chickens are there now in the shed?

e. 12 budgies are singing in a large cage. Next to them, in another cage, there are 20 budgies who are fast asleep. How many budgies are there altogether?

f. Toby counted 36 stripes on one zebra and 33 stripes on another zebra. How many stripes did Toby count altogether?

g. There are 300 windows in one building and 250 windows in the building across the road. How many windows are there altogether?

h. Ziggy loves penguins. When he travelled to the Antarctic, he counted 241 penguins on the first day and 142 penguins on the second day. How many penguins did he see altogether on both days?

i.   Simon did 46 press-ups and Sally did 52 press-ups. How many more press-ups did Sally manage? How many press-ups did Simon and Sally do altogether?

j.   Early in the morning there were 400 sheep in the field. In the afternoon another 140 sheep joined them. A few hours later 4 more sheep came along. How many sheep were there altogether?

❧ LESSON **THIRTY-FOUR** ❧

Introduce the addition of three-digit numbers with 'carrying on' from the units column to the tens column and with 'carrying on' from the tens column to the hundreds column.

EXAMPLE:

```
  176
+ 349
─────
  525
─────
1 1 (carried over)
```

1. Write down the following sums and give the correct answers, showing the working-out clearly:

TAKE CARE TO WRITE EACH NUMERAL IN THE CORRECT COLUMN

a.
```
  444
 + 48
─────

─────
```

b.
```
  656
+ 154
─────

─────
```

c.
```
  202
 + 28
─────

─────
```

d.
```
  550
 + 55
─────

─────
```

e. $\begin{array}{r} 909 \\ +26 \\ \hline \\ \hline \end{array}$

f. $\begin{array}{r} 616 \\ +84 \\ \hline \\ \hline \end{array}$

g. $\begin{array}{r} 46 \\ +564 \\ \hline \\ \hline \end{array}$

h. $\begin{array}{r} 801 \\ +108 \\ \hline \\ \hline \end{array}$

i. $\begin{array}{r} 361 \\ +339 \\ \hline \\ \hline \end{array}$

j. $\begin{array}{r} 108 \\ + 802 \\ \hline \\ \hline \end{array}$

2. **Write down the following sums and give the correct answers, setting each sum out in the correct columns:**

   a. **406 + 64 =**

   b. **38 + 380 =**

   c. **5 + 505 =**

   d. **101 + 110 =**

   e. **22 + 220 =**

   f. **648 + 96 =**

g. **567 + 94 =**

h. **766 + 154 =**

i. **88 + 184 =**

j. **10 + 110 =**

3. **Write down the following sums and give the correct answers, showing the working-out clearly, with each numeral in the correct column:**

a. **My pet rabbit hops 48 times and then he hops another 26 times. How many times has he hopped altogether?**

b. **Coco counted 56 tiles on one side of the roof. Afterwards she counted another 39 tiles on the other side of the roof. How many tiles did Coco count altogether?**

c. **Mandy saw 35 swimmers in the sea. If another 45 swimmers joined them, how many swimmers were there altogether in the sea?**

d. **A flock of 39 birds flew over the trees and then another 24 birds followed. How many birds altogether flew over the trees?**

e. **Jed counted 224 stars in the sky. His sister counted another 186 stars. How many stars did they count altogether?**

f. **Sheba the shark ate 128 fish one morning. In the afternoon she ate another 67 fish. How many fish did Sheba eat altogether?**

g. **Candy put 136 pebbles in a bucket. Her brother added another 175 pebbles. How many pebbles are there altogether in the bucket?**

h. **Mr Pocket sold 138 shirts on Monday and 283 shirts on Tuesday. How many shirts did Mr Pocket sell altogether on both Monday and Tuesday?**

i. **There are 263 apples on the**

counter. Alex added another 158 apples. How many apples are there altogether on the counter?

j. Miss Gold has a box of buttons. She counts 323 buttons. Miss Silver has another box of buttons in which there are 468 buttons. How many buttons do Miss Gold and Miss Silver have altogether?

❧ LESSON **THIRTY-FIVE** ❧

Introduce the subtraction of a three-digit number from another three-digit number 'without borrowing'.

EXAMPLE:

```
   467
 − 143
 ─────
   324
 ═════
```

1. Write down the following sums and give the correct answers, showing the working-out clearly:

TAKE CARE TO WRITE EACH NUMERAL IN THE CORRECT COLUMN

a.
```
   894
 − 102
 ─────

 ─────
```

b.
```
   683
 − 42
 ─────

 ─────
```

c.
```
   480
 − 40
 ─────

 ─────
```

d.
```
   500
 − 300
 ─────

 ─────
```

e.
```
   198
 − 111
 ─────

 ─────
```

f.
```
   346
 − 31
 ─────

 ─────
```

g.
$$777$$
$$-77$$
_____

_____

h.
$$265$$
$$-55$$
_____

_____

i.
$$444$$
$$-303$$
_____

_____

j.
$$909$$
$$-101$$
_____

_____

2. **Write down the following sums and give the correct answers, setting each sum out in the correct columns:**

    a. **48 − 32 =**

    b. **999 − 111 =**

    c. **836 − 15 =**

    d. **404 − 102 =**

    e. **765 − 52 =**

    f. **806 − 4 =**

    g. **398 − 18 =**

    h. **639 − 26 =**

    i. **909 − 101 =**

    j. **999 − 111 =**

3. **Write down the following sums and give the correct answers, showing the working-out clearly, with each numeral in the correct column:**

   a. Take 300 away from 500.

   b. There were 200 cows in the field. 100 cows were led back to the shed. How many cows were left in the field?

   c. On Friday 150 pupils of the 250 pupils who are usually at school were away. How many pupils were at school on Friday?

   d. There are 330 tissues in a box. If Sophia uses 20 of them, how many tissues will be left in the box?

   e. Yolanda put 271 jelly beans into a jar. Her little brother ate 30 of them. How many jelly beans were left in the jar?

   f. The car park at the end of my road has 286 spaces for cars. Yesterday there were 25 empty spaces. How many cars were in the car park yesterday?

g. There are 163 elephants in the safari park. If 41 of these elephants were moved to the zoo, how many elephants would remain in the safari park?

h. Samantha invited 121 friends to her birthday party. Unfortunately, 11 of them could not come. How many friends came to her party?

i. On Wednesday there were 545 leaves on the tree at the end of my garden. If 34 leaves fall from the tree every day, how many leaves were on the tree the day after Wednesday? How many leaves were on the tree on Friday?

j. There are 39 steps at the end of my garden. A frog jumps 2 steps every hour. How many steps will the frog have jumped after 2 hours? How

**many steps must the frog still jump
if he wants to jump up all the stairs?**

❧ LESSON **THIRTY-SIX** ❧

Introduce the subtraction of a three-digit number from another three-digit number 'with borrowing'. Initially, children should practise 'borrowing' only from the hundreds column. (See Lesson Thirty-Seven, when 'borrowing' will be extended to include both the tens and the hundreds column, and subtracting from three-digit numbers with **0** in the tens column.)

EXAMPLE:

$$
\begin{array}{r}
^6\!\!\not{7}\,^1 2\ 7 \\
-\ 1\ 4\ 3 \\
\hline
5\ 8\ 4 \\
\hline
\end{array}
$$

1. Write down the following sums and work out the correct answers, showing clearly the one hundred that has been 'borrowed' from the hundreds column to be added to the tens column:

a.
$$
\begin{array}{r}
824 \\
-142 \\
\hline
\\
\hline
\end{array}
$$

b.
$$
\begin{array}{r}
633 \\
-242 \\
\hline
\\
\hline
\end{array}
$$

c.
$$
\begin{array}{r}
440 \\
-140 \\
\hline
\\
\hline
\end{array}
$$

d.
$$
\begin{array}{r}
512 \\
-391 \\
\hline
\\
\hline
\end{array}
$$

e.   788
     − 191
     _____

     _____

f.   846
     − 351
     _____

     _____

g.   777
     − 287
     _____

     _____

h.   655
     − 375
     _____

     _____

i.   444
     − 163
     _____

     _____

j.   919
     − 121
     _____

     _____

2. **Write down the following sums and give the correct answers, setting each sum out in the correct columns and showing clearly the number 'borrowed' from the hundreds column to be transferred to the tens column:**

   a. **333 − 192 =**

   b. **645 − 252 =**

   c. **738 − 296 =**

   d. **831 − 440 =**

e. **555 − 362 =**

f. **913 − 671 =**

g. **453 − 262 =**

h. **910 − 330 =**

i. **363 − 171 =**

j. **555 − 262 =**

3. **Write down the following numbers in order from the smallest to the largest, and then subtract the smallest number from the largest number:**

148, 319, 452, 616, 829, 269, 739.

❧ LESSON **THIRTY-SEVEN** ❧

Introduce the subtraction of a three-digit number from another three-digit number 'with borrowing' both from the hundreds and tens column.

EXAMPLE:

$$\begin{array}{r} {}^{6}\!7\,{}^{12}3\,{}^{1}4 \\ -\,1\ 4\ 5 \\ \hline 5\ 8\ 9 \\ \hline \end{array}$$

Note: it is at this point that children should learn how to approach subtraction 'with borrowing' when there is a zero in the tens column and insufficient units in the units column; in such cases, one 'borrows' from the hundreds column to the tens column and then from the tens column to the units column before any subtraction takes place.

EXAMPLE:

$$\begin{array}{r} {}^{9} \\ {}^{6}\!7\,{}^{1}0\,{}^{1}3 \\ -\,1\ 4\ 7 \\ \hline 5\ 5\ 6 \\ \hline \end{array}$$

1. Write down the following sums and work out the correct answers, showing clearly the one hundred that has been 'borrowed' from the hundreds column to be added to the tens column and the ten that has been

'borrowed' from the tens column to be added to the units column:

a.
$$753$$
$$-166$$

b.
$$645$$
$$-156$$

c.
$$776$$
$$-438$$

d.
$$665$$
$$-279$$

e.
$$876$$
$$-489$$

f.
$$812$$
$$-283$$

g.
$$742$$
$$-497$$

h.
$$811$$
$$-222$$

i.
$$851$$
$$-345$$

j.
$$751$$
$$-483$$

2. **Write down the following sums and give the correct answers, setting each sum out in the correct columns and showing clearly the number 'borrowed' from the hundreds column to be transferred to the tens column and the number 'borrowed' from the tens column to be transferred to the units column:**

    a. **753 − 476 =**

    b. **864 − 359 =**

    c. **432 − 299 =**

    d. **324 − 176 =**

    e. **843 − 561 =**

    f. **537 − 379 =**

    g. **761 − 498 =**

    h. **481 − 297 =**

    i. **567 − 389 =**

    j. **623 − 276 =**

3. **Subtract the smallest number from the largest number:**

   724, 198, 236, 189, 742

4. **Write down the following sums with 0 in the tens column and work out the correct answers, showing clearly the** one hundred **that has been 'borrowed' from the hundreds column to be added to the tens column and the** ten **that has been 'borrowed' from the tens column to be added to the units column:**

   a. $\begin{array}{r} 503 \\ -128 \\ \hline \\ \hline \end{array}$

   b. $\begin{array}{r} 804 \\ -217 \\ \hline \\ \hline \end{array}$

   c. $\begin{array}{r} 906 \\ -637 \\ \hline \\ \hline \end{array}$

   d. $\begin{array}{r} 303 \\ -139 \\ \hline \\ \hline \end{array}$

   e. $\begin{array}{r} 404 \\ -145 \\ \hline \\ \hline \end{array}$

   f. $\begin{array}{r} 402 \\ -243 \\ \hline \\ \hline \end{array}$

g.   707
      − 279
      ‾‾‾‾

h.   605
      − 156
      ‾‾‾‾

i.   308
      − 169
      ‾‾‾‾

j.   903
      − 187
      ‾‾‾‾

5. **Write down the following sums with 0 in the tens column and give the correct answers, setting each sum out in the correct columns and showing clearly the number 'borrowed' from the hundreds column to be transferred to the tens column and the number 'borrowed' to be transferred to the units column:**

    a.   **604 − 145 =**

    b.   **708 − 299 =**

    c.   **403 − 264 =**

    d.   **304 − 116 =**

    e.   **502 − 255 =**

    f.   **902 − 777 =**

g. **803 − 667 =**

h. **207 − 148 =**

i. **605 − 489 =**

j. **706 − 677 =**

6. **Subtract the smallest number from the largest number:**

   503, 505, 166, 404, 156, 501

7. **Write down the following sums and give the correct answers, showing the working-out clearly, with each numeral in the correct column:**

   a. **There are 302 ribbons in a box. If Solo takes out 46 ribbons, how many ribbons will remain in the box?**

   b. **If Pringle takes 23 crisps out of a packet of crisps and there were 124 crisps in the packet to start with, how many crisps will be left in the packet?**

c.   **334 dancers are on stage. If 119 of them leave the stage, how many dancers will remain on stage?**

d.   **On a clear night Bombo sees 204 stars. A cloud appears and covers up 36 stars. How many stars can Bombo now see?**

e.   **Ted loves chocolates. He sees 401 chocolates in a huge box of chocolates. If he eats 12 chocolates, how many chocolates will be left in the box?**

f.   **A jigsaw puzzle has 404 pieces. If Fran loses 17 pieces of the puzzle, how many pieces will be left?**

g.   **Nikita draws 303 dots on a sheet of paper. She rubs out 116 of them. How many dots remain on the sheet of paper?**

h.   **55 birds land on a tree. If 27 of them fly away, how many birds will be left on the tree?**

i. It is autumn and the leaves are falling from the trees. Seraphina counts 305 leaves on the tree early in the morning. When she comes home in the evening, she counts only 126. How many leaves have fallen from the tree during the day while Seraphina has been away?

j. Dax loves collecting marbles. He has 405 marbles. His friend, Pronto, also loves collecting marbles and he only has 10 marbles. Dax chooses 128 marbles from his collection and gives them to Pronto as a present. How many marbles does Pronto now have? How many marbles does Dax have left?

❦ LESSON **THIRTY-EIGHT** ❦

Introduce the addition of three-digit numbers that ought to be written down in vertical columns. Now, strings of numbers can be added in three columns and in three, four or more rows. It is imperative that digits are placed exactly in the units, tens or hundreds column.

EXAMPLE:

$50 + 567 + 48 + 109 =$

$$
\begin{array}{r}
50 \\
567 \\
48 \\
+109 \\
\hline
774 \\
\hline
\end{array}
$$
1 2 (carried over)

Note: the amount 'carried over' varies; when adding three rows of numbers, either nothing is to be 'carried' or **1** or **2** will be 'carried'. The greater the number of rows, the greater the number that may be 'carried'. For example, adding 99 + 99 + 99 + 99 results in the 'carrying' of **3**.

1. Write down the following sums and give the correct answers, showing the working-out clearly:

TAKE CARE TO WRITE EACH NUMERAL IN THE CORRECT COLUMN

a.
```
  406
   12
+111
_____

_____
```

b.
```
   94
   13
+413
_____

_____
```

c.
```
  887
   78
  + 3
_____

_____
```

d.
```
  303
   30
+333
_____

_____
```

e.
```
  515
   15
 +90
_____

_____
```

f.
```
   24
   36
 +91
_____

_____
```

g.
```
  801
  108
 +81
_____

_____
```

h.
```
  201
   21
+288
_____

_____
```

i.
```
  446
  106
 +72
_____

_____
```

j.
```
  639
   93
+133
_____

_____
```

2.   **Write down the following sums and give the correct answers, setting each sum out in the correct columns:**

Note: preferably, numbers should be written down in the order in which they appear, rather than from largest to smallest.

a.   **480 + 39 + 13 =**

b.   **4 + 116 + 203 =**

c.   **13 + 313 + 33 =**

d.   **900 + 9 + 90 =**

e.   **708 + 77 + 87 =**

f.   **96 + 389 + 108 =**

g.   **408 + 82 + 20 =**

h.   **63 + 306 + 246 =**

i.   **200 + 20 + 222 =**

j.   **88 + 81 + 688 =**

3.   **Now do these sums and show all the working-out:**

a.   **Robby sold 262 Christmas cards on**

Monday, 310 cards on Tuesday and 64 cards on Wednesday. How many Christmas cards did Robby sell on all three days? How many cards did he sell altogether on Monday and Wednesday?

b. Zak and his brothers sell cars. Last year they sold 460 cars and this year they only sold 49 cars. How many cars did they sell altogether?

c. Serena buys peanuts in large quantities. She bought a packet of 550 peanuts last week and another packet of 405 peanuts this week. How many peanuts did she buy altogether?

d. Finn works in a florist. Yesterday she sold 400 roses and today she sold 350 roses. How many roses has she sold altogether?

e. The Internet Cycle Company sells lots of bicycles. On Thursday it sold 82 bicycles, on Friday it sold 28 bicycles and on Saturday it sold 181 bicycles. How many bicycles did the Internet Cycle Company sell on Thursday and Saturday? How many bicycles altogether did it sell on Thursday, Friday and Saturday?

f.   Tilly, Milly and Billy sell more houses than anyone else in the world. Last year they sold 330 houses and so far this year they have sold 222 houses. How many houses have they sold since the beginning of last year?

g.   There are 660 caravans in the caravan park. 340 more caravans arrive. How many caravans are there now in the caravan park?

h.   Bo makes hats. Last year she made 135 hats and the year before she made 165 hats. How many hats altogether did Bo make last year and the year before?

i. Donna counts 123 stars in the night sky. Her brother, Joshua, counts another 187 stars. How many stars altogether have Donna and Joshua counted?

j. Toby stacks shelves in the supermarket. He puts 300 tins of baked beans, 400 tins of spaghetti and 142 tins of peaches on one shelf. How many tins of baked beans and peaches has Toby stacked on this shelf? How many tins of spaghetti and peaches has Toby stacked on this shelf? How many tins altogether has he stacked on this shelf?

Introduce the classification of odd and even numbers. Numbers that end in **0**, **2**, **4**, **6** or **8** are even numbers; numbers that end in **1**, **3**, **5**, **7** or **9** are odd numbers.

1. **Which of the following numbers are odd and which are even:**

   121, 642, 666, 912, 842, 132, 181, 80, 801, 87, 990, 110, 85, 580, 123

2. **Make the largest possible odd number by placing the following digits in the appropriate columns:**

   a. **2, 5, 1**

   b. **3, 6, 8**

   c. **1, 2, 7**

   d. **5, 7, 1**

3. **Make the smallest possible even number by placing the following digits in the appropriate columns:**

   a. **4, 6, 5**

    b. **8, 2, 3**

    c. **3, 1, 4**

    d. **9, 7, 8**

    e. **7, 3, 2**

4. **Write down the following in numerals:**

    a. **One hundred and eleven**

    b. **Nine hundred and ten**

    c. **Four hundred and forty**

    d. **One hundred and eleven**

    e. **Ninety-nine**

5. **Write down these numbers in order from the smallest to the largest:**

    a. **101, 110, 111, 11, 100, 10**

    b. **545, 555, 45, 54, 55, 505**

    c. **91, 99, 19, 119, 911, 191**

    d. **34, 403, 333, 343, 433**

    e. **77, 707, 607, 67, 777, 76, 706**

6. **Write down these numbers in order from the largest to the smallest:**

    a.   **200, 120, 221, 201, 102, 122**

    b.   **404, 440, 44, 444, 441, 41**

    c.   **10, 100, 101, 111, 110, 11**

    d.   **55, 505, 59, 550, 50, 5**

    e.   **660, 606, 66, 96, 906, 69**

❦ LESSON **FORTY** ❦

Introduce multiplication and the sign (✗) that denotes it. Multiplication should be understood as a 'compact' form of adding together the same number repeatedly, so that **2 + 2 + 2** may be 'compacted' as **3 × 2** and **10 + 10 + 10 + 10 + 10** may be 'compacted' as **5 × 10**.

These groupings of different amounts of the same number constitute arithmetical tables, which should in due course be memorised up to the **12×** table. Since our number system is decimal, many prefer to omit the **11×** and **12×** tables. However, time is invariably calculated in patterns of twelve, and so it is most helpful to be familiar with the **12×** table, in particular.

Note: does **2 × 10** mean two groups of ten or ten groups of two? Strictly speaking, it is two groups of ten. It is helpful to interpret the multiplication sign as a symbol denoting the word 'of' so that **100 × 101** means one hundred lots of one hundred and one, which is to say it lies in the **101** times table! It is of interest to note the difference between **0 × 10** and **10 × 0**; the former means no lots of ten, the latter means ten lots of nothing. Obviously, the answer to both sums is **0**.

This is the **10×** table:

1 × 10 = 10	5 × 10 = 50	9 × 10 = 90
2 × 10 = 20	6 × 10 = 60	10 × 10 = 100
3 × 10 = 30	7 × 10 = 70	11 × 10 = 110
4 × 10 = 40	8 × 10 = 80	12 × 10 = 120

Needless to say, its ease lies in the fact that one simply adds 0 to the multiplier.

Multiplication tables should be memorised; however, it is futile to memorise only the multiples of ten without multiplier and multiplicand. On no account should children say **10, 20, 30, 40**, etc.

(See the Guidelines at the beginning of this book for further discussion of the memorisation of multiplication tables.)

WITH THE COMMENCEMENT OF THIS CHAPTER IT IS NOW APPROPRIATE TO MEMORISE THE 10x TABLE.

1. **Write down the following sums and insert the correct answers in the space provided:**

    a. ..... × 10 = 40

    b. ..... × 10 = 110

    c. 5 × ..... = 50

    d. 0 × 10 = ...

    e. 7 × ..... = 70

    f. 12 × ..... = 120

    g. 2 × ..... = 20

h. **8 × 10 = ...**

i. **..... × 10 = 90**

j. **3 × ..... = 30**

2. **Using the 10× table, work out the answers to the following problems:**

   a. **There are 10 silver stars in one packet. Aunty Flo buys 10 packets. How many silver stars will she have altogether?**

   b. **Biff buys 6 packets of rulers. There are 10 rulers in each packet. How many rulers did he buy?**

   c. **On Monday morning the policewoman took 9 groups of 10 children across the road. How many children did she lead across the road on Monday morning?**

   d. **Danny reads 10 pages of his book every night before he goes to sleep. If he does this for 5 nights, how many pages of his book does he read?**

e.   Lola buys 6 packets of stickers. Each packet has 10 stickers in it. How many stickers does she have?

f.   If Hugo buys 9 boxes of pencils and each box contains 10 pencils, how many pencils does Hugo have altogether?

g.   Mum loves scented soap. She buys 4 packets with 10 bars of soap in each packet. How many bars of soap does she buy altogether?

h.   Jed looks out of the window and counts cars whizzing by. Every time 10 cars pass by, he puts a mark on a piece of paper. How many cars have passed by when there are 5 marks on the paper?

i.   There are 8 boxes of crystal glasses on the shelf. If there are 10 crystal glasses in each box, how many crystal glasses are there altogether?

j.   **Bobby collects football cards. If he has 12 sets of ten cards, how many cards does he have altogether?**

PONTI PANDA IN THE SUPERSTORE

Many years ago there were lots of little shops on the High Street. There was a baker who sold loaves of bread, a butcher with cuts of meat in the window, a grocer who sold tea from faraway India and coffee from Brazil. A favourite shop, of course, was the sweet shop with jars of mints, fruit drops and chocolate drops; as for Dad, he always stopped at the newspaper shop to buy his paper.

Nowadays all these shops are found in one place called a superstore. The displays in the window show that you can buy almost anything in the local superstore. One fine day Ponti Panda pressed his nose against the window and peered in. He just had to see inside! Late one night he slipped in and hid among the furry animals on sale for Christmas until the store was empty. Fortunately, the store was well lit and an assistant was stacking the shelves. Ponti Panda could see everything that was going on. The superstore was full of colour and variety and lots and lots of packets, tins, jars and cartons. Golden jars of honey caught his eye. There were so many of them and Ponti Panda decided to count them all. But he could not manage to keep the big numbers in his head and he was distracted by all the other jam jars and baked-bean tins and yoghurt pots. He got to the number 52 and had to start again. He tried putting little dots on a piece of paper but after a while he got completely mixed up. How could he count more easily?

Well, thought Ponti, the number 10 was easy to

remember. What if he drew one little line for every ten jars of honey? That way five lines would stand for fifty jars and six lines would stand for sixty jars. Ten lines would mean that there were one hundred jars of honey on the shelf.

And so he counted and drew his little pencil lines and hummed to himself and discovered that there were fifty jars of golden honey on the shelf. What a great game Ponti had invented for himself. He had also discovered that counting in groups, which is called multiplication, makes adding numbers quick and easy. Instead of adding all the way up to one hundred, he could divide everything into groups of ten and multiply. And so Ponti Panda discovered the ten times table:

$$1 \times 10 = 10$$

$$2 \times 10 = 20$$

$$3 \times 10 = 30$$

$$4 \times 10 = 40$$

$$5 \times 10 = 50$$

$$6 \times 10 = 60$$

$$7 \times 10 = 70$$

$$8 \times 10 = 80$$

$$9 \times 10 = 90$$

$$10 \times 10 = 100$$

$$11 \times 10 = 110$$

$$12 \times 10 = 120$$

As Ponti wandered through the store he found that some bottles were packed in cartons of five. So two cartons of five made ten bottles and three cartons of five made fifteen bottles. This, Ponti now realised, was the five times table which he hadn't learned yet.

❧ LESSON **FORTY-ONE** ❧

Introduce the **5×** table. This is a 'compact' form of adding together so that **5 + 5 + 5 = 3 × 5**, and so on.

This is the **5×** table:

$1 \times 5 = 5$	$5 \times 5 = 25$	$9 \times 5 = 45$
$2 \times 5 = 10$	$6 \times 5 = 30$	$10 \times 5 = 50$
$3 \times 5 = 15$	$7 \times 5 = 35$	$11 \times 5 = 55$
$4 \times 5 = 20$	$8 \times 5 = 40$	$12 \times 5 = 60$

Note: multiplication tables should be memorised; however, it is futile to memorise only the multiples of five without multiplier and multiplicand. On no account should children say **5, 10, 15, 20, 25**, etc.

(See the Guidelines at the beginning of this book for further discussion of the memorisation of multiplication tables.)

WITH THE COMMENCEMENT OF THIS CHAPTER IT IS NOW APPROPRIATE TO MEMORISE THE 5x TABLE.

1. **Write down the following multiplication sums with the correct answers:**

    a. **$6 \times 5 =$**

    b. **$7 \times 5 =$**

c. $8 \times 5 =$

d. $3 \times 5 =$

e. $10 \times 5 =$

f. $5 \times 10 =$

g. $11 \times 5 =$

h. $9 \times 5 =$

i. $2 \times 5 =$

j. $12 \times 5 =$

2. **Write out the following sums and insert the correct answers in the space provided:**

a. $..... \times 5 = 40$

b. $..... \times 5 = 60$

c. $5 \times ..... = 50$

d. $0 \times 5 = ...$

e. $7 \times ..... = 35$

f. $12 \times ..... = 60$

g. $2 \times \ldots = 10$

h. $9 \times 5 = \ldots$

i. $\ldots \times 5 = 55$

j. $3 \times \ldots = 15$

k. $\ldots \times 10 = 40$

l. $\ldots \times 10 = 120$

m. $0 \times 10 = \ldots$

n. $12 \times \ldots = 120$

o. $\ldots \times 3 = 15$

p. $9 \times 5 = \ldots$

q. $9 \times 10 = \ldots$

r. $\ldots \times 5 = 55$

s. $3 \times \ldots = 30$

t. $35 = \ldots \times 5$

3. Using the 5× and 10× tables, work out the answers to the following problems. Do not work out the answers by writing down adding sums.

   a. There are 12 jars of jelly beans on the shelf. If each jar contains 10 jelly beans, how many jelly beans are there altogether?

   b. There are 10 potatoes in each bag of potatoes. Lulu buys 7 bags. How many potatoes has Lulu bought?

   c. Jodi loves conkers. She collects 10 conkers on Friday, 10 on Saturday and another 10 on Sunday. How many conkers does she have altogether?

   d. Granny cooks fairy cakes and puts them into pretty boxes to give as presents. If she puts 7 cakes in each box, how many cakes would she need to fill 5 boxes?

   e. Lara goes to the supermarket and

buys 5 packets of biscuits. If each packet has 12 biscuits, how many biscuits does she buy?

f. There are 6 party poppers in each bag. If Tina buys 10 bags, how many party poppers does she have?

g. There are 9 piles of newspapers on the table. If each pile has 10 newspapers, how many newspapers are there altogether?

h. If Jake reads 3 magazines every day for 5 days, how many magazines has Jake read altogether?

i. If Mum puts 8 chocolate brownies on 5 plates, how many chocolate brownies are there altogether?

j. There are 12 packets of envelopes on my desk. If there are 10 envelopes in each packet, how many envelopes are there altogether on my desk?

❧ LESSON **FORTY-TWO** ❧

Introduce the **2×** table. This is a 'compact' form of adding together so that **2 + 2 + 2 = 3 × 2**, and so on. At this point, one should explain what is meant by 'a pair'.

This is the **2×** table:

$1 \times 2 = 2$	$5 \times 2 = 10$	$9 \times 2 = 18$
$2 \times 2 = 4$	$6 \times 2 = 12$	$10 \times 2 = 20$
$3 \times 2 = 6$	$7 \times 2 = 14$	$11 \times 2 = 22$
$4 \times 2 = 8$	$8 \times 2 = 16$	$12 \times 2 = 24$

Note: multiplication tables should be memorised; however, it is futile to memorise only the multiples of two without multiplier and multiplicand. On no account should children say **2, 4, 6, 8, 10**, etc. This is particularly important in respect of the **2×** table where it is relatively easy to add up in twos and double numbers. For example, children should not simply say **14**; they should say that **7 × 2 = 14** or that **14 = 7 × 2**.

(See the Guidelines at the beginning of this book for further discussion of the memorisation of multiplication tables.)

WITH THE COMMENCEMENT OF THIS CHAPTER IT IS NOW APPROPRIATE TO MEMORISE THE 2x TABLE.

1. **Write down the following multiplication sums with the correct answers:**

    a. **6 × 2 =**

    b. **7 × 2 =**

    c. **8 × 2 =**

    d. **3 × 2 =**

    e. **10 × 2 =**

    f. **5 × 2 =**

    g. **11 × 2 =**

    h. **9 × 2 =**

    i. **2 × 2 =**

    j. **12 × 2 =**

2. **Write out the following sums and insert the correct answers in the space provided:**

    a. **..... × 2 = 20**

    b. **..... × 2 = 24**

    c. **5 × ..... = 10**

d. $0 \times 2 =$ .....

e. $7 \times$ ..... $= 14$

f. $12 \times$ ..... $= 24$

g. $2 \times$ ..... $= 4$

h. $9 \times 2 =$ .....

i. ..... $\times 2 = 22$

j. $3 \times$ ..... $= 6$

k. ..... $\times 10 = 110$

l. ..... $\times 5 = 55$

m. $0 \times 5 =$ .....

n. $12 \times$ ..... $= 60$

o. ..... $\times 3 = 30$

p. $9 \times 10 =$ .....

q. $9 \times 5 =$ .....

r. ..... $\times 5 = 50$

s. $3 \times$ ..... $= 15$

t. $45 =$ ..... $\times 5$

3. **Copy out the following sums and put the correct number in the empty box. Remember that the 'equals' sign means 'the same as'.**

   a. $2 \times 10 = 4 \times \square$

   b. $12 \times \square = 6 \times 2$

   c. $2 \times \square = 5 \times 2$

   d. $3 \times 10 = 6 \times \square$

   e. $8 \times 5 = \square \times 10$

   f. $6 \times 10 = 12 \times \square$

   g. $\square \times 10 = 2 \times 5$

   h. $4 \times 5 = \square \times 2$

   i. $1 \times \square = 6 \times 2$

   j. $\square \times 10 = 90 + 10$

4. **Using the multiplication tables that you have learned so far, work out the answers to the following problems. Do not work out the answers by writing down adding sums. Remember that numbers may be expressed in numerals or in words.**

a. **Bubbles went shopping and bought 5 bags of lemons. If there were 2 lemons in each bag, how many lemons did she buy?**

b. **A class of children walked to the park two by two. If the teacher counted 11 pairs of children, how many children walked to the park?**

c. **If Maggie hangs 12 pairs of socks on the washing line, how many pegs will she need to hold them one by one?**

d. **Zak was cleaning shoes. If he had to clean 6 pairs of shoes, how many single shoes did he clean altogether?**

e. **If Fran bought 7 ice-creams with 2 scoops of ice-cream on each ice-cream cone, how many scoops of ice-cream were there altogether?**

f. **Jenny loves sweet tea. If she drinks 8 cups in one day and if she puts 2** spoons of sugar in each cup, how many spoons of sugar did she use altogether?

g. Sammy loved honey so much that he helped himself to 2 spoonfuls of honey every time he saw the jar of honey that his mother kept on the kitchen table. If he opened the jar 6 times in one day, how many spoonfuls of honey did he eat?

h. If there are 9 desks in the library and there are 2 books on each desk, how many books are there altogether on the desks in the library?

i. If Zig and Zag visited 9 planets and left 2 flags on each planet, how many flags did they leave altogether?

j. If 2 children enter the playground every 5 minutes, how many children will be in the playground after 10 minutes?

❦ LESSON **FORTY-THREE** ❦

Introduce division and the sign (÷) that denotes it, using the **2×**, **5×** and **10×** tables. Division is the inverse of multiplication. It is the means by which one discovers how many groups or lots of the same quantity there are in any given number.

Division can be learned alongside multiplication, as follows:

$1 \times 10 = 10$	→	$10 \div 10 = 1$
$2 \times 10 = 20$	→	$20 \div 10 = 2$
$3 \times 10 = 30$	→	$30 \div 10 = 3$
$4 \times 10 = 40$	→	$40 \div 10 = 4$
$5 \times 10 = 50$	→	$50 \div 10 = 5$
$6 \times 10 = 60$	→	$60 \div 10 = 6$
$7 \times 10 = 70$	→	$70 \div 10 = 7$
$8 \times 10 = 80$	→	$80 \div 10 = 8$
$9 \times 10 = 90$	→	$90 \div 10 = 9$
$10 \times 10 = 100$	→	$100 \div 10 = 10$
$11 \times 10 = 110$	→	$110 \div 10 = 11$
$12 \times 10 = 120$	→	$120 \div 10 = 12$

Needless to say, the ease of dividing by ten is that one simply removes **0** from the dividend just as, in multiplication by ten, one adds **0** to the multiplier. Once one has learned the **10×** table, it should be relatively easy – and it is most advantageous – to learn this arithmetical table in its dividing form.

Note: whereas both addition and multiplication are commutative (**10 + 5 = 5 + 10** and **5 × 10 = 10 × 5**), neither subtraction nor division are commutative (**10 − 5 ≠ 5 − 10** and **10 ÷ 5 ≠ 5 ÷ 10**).

1. **Write down the following division sums with the correct answers:**

    a. **$50 \div 10 =$**

    b. **$60 \div 10 =$**

    c. **$30 \div 10 =$**

    d. **$80 \div 10 =$**

    e. **$90 \div 10 =$**

    f. **$70 \div 10 =$**

    g. **$40 \div 10 =$**

    h. **$110 \div 10 =$**

    i. **$120 \div 10 =$**

    j. **$10 \div 10 =$**

2. **Now answer the following questions:**

    a. **What is 60 divided by 10?**

    b. **What is 90 divided by 10?**

    c. **Zen has 50 marbles which he wants to divide equally among 10 boys. How many marbles should he give each boy?**

d. **Mum cuts a large birthday cake into 20 slices. If there are 10 children at the party and she wants to share out the cake equally, how many slices of birthday cake does each child receive?**

e. **If Kit shares 80 stickers equally between her 10 friends, how many stickers does each friend get?**

f. **30 packets of crisps are shared equally between 10 boys. How many packets of crisps does each boy receive?**

g. **Ruby has to pack 60 potatoes in lots of 10. How many lots will she have?**

h. **There are 120 apples in a box. If a farmer puts the same number of apples into 10 bags, how many apples must be put into each bag?**

i. **Mrs Donut has 110 pencils. If she wants to share them equally among 10 children, how many pencils will each child receive?**

j.   Jenny puts 90 jars of honey into boxes. Each box fits 10 jars of honey. If she fills every box, how many boxes of honey will she have?

3.   Copy out the following sums and put the correct number in the empty box:

a. $10 \div 10 = 1 \times \square$

b. $10 \times \square = 100 \div 10$

c. $40 \div 10 = 2 \times \square$

d. $70 \div 10 = 5 + \square$

e. $120 \div \square = 7 + 5$

f. $\square \div 10 = 15 - 4$

g. $20 \div \square = 2 \times 10$

h. $80 \div 10 = \square \times 2$

i. $3 \times 10 = \square \times 5$

j. $8 \times 5 = \square \times 10$

❧ LESSON **FORTY-FOUR** ❧

Revise the **5x** table and introduce division by **5**.

1 × 5 = 5	→	5 ÷ 5 = 1
2 × 5 = 10	→	10 ÷ 5 = 2
3 × 5 = 15	→	15 ÷ 5 = 3
4 × 5 = 20	→	20 ÷ 5 = 4
5 × 5 = 25	→	25 ÷ 5 = 5
6 × 5 = 30	→	30 ÷ 5 = 6
7 × 5 = 35	→	35 ÷ 5 = 7
8 × 5 = 40	→	40 ÷ 5 = 8
9 × 5 = 45	→	45 ÷ 5 = 9
10 × 5 = 50	→	50 ÷ 5 = 10
11 × 5 = 55	→	55 ÷ 5 = 11
12 × 5 = 60	→	60 ÷ 5 = 12

1. Write down the following division sums with the correct answers:

a. **50 ÷ 5 =**

b. **10 ÷ 5 =**

c. **20 ÷ 5 =**

d. **40 ÷ 5 =**

e. **60 ÷ 5 =**

f. $5 \div 5 =$

g. $15 \div 5 =$

h. $30 \div 5 =$

i. $35 \div 5 =$

j. $55 \div 5 =$

2. **Now answer the following questions:**

   a. **Sam has 40 Christmas crackers and 4 friends. If he divided the crackers equally between himself and his 4 friends, how many crackers will each of them have?**

   b. **There are 60 books on the teacher's table and she asks Mandy to stack them in equal piles with 5 books in each pile. How many piles will there be on the teacher's desk?**

   c. **If 1 box holds 5 ties and I have 25 ties to pack, how many boxes do I need?**

   d. **Mum asks Felix to divide 50 cubes**

of sugar into bowls with 5 cubes in each bowl. How many bowls will Felix need?

e. If a florist needs to divide 45 roses equally between 5 people, how many roses will each person receive?

f. If 55 packets of tea are sent to 11 people so that each person receives exactly the same number of packets, how many packets will each person receive?

g. If 40 ribbons are shared equally among 5 girls, how many ribbons will each girl receive?

h. If 35 folders are shared equally between 5 teachers, how many folders will each teacher get?

i. If Serena has 25 cards and there are 5 players, how many cards must she give each player if each player has the same number of cards?

j. **Kim collects shells and decides to share them with her friends. She finds 4 empty boxes on the beach. If she fills each box with 5 shells, how many shells did she have to start with?**

❦ LESSON **FORTY-FIVE** ❦

Revise the **2x** table and introduce division by **2**.

1 × 2 = 2	→	2 ÷ 2 = 1
2 × 2 = 4	→	4 ÷ 2 = 2
3 × 2 = 6	→	6 ÷ 2 = 3
4 × 2 = 8	→	8 ÷ 2 = 4
5 × 2 = 10	→	10 ÷ 2 = 5
6 × 2 = 12	→	12 ÷ 2 = 6
7 × 2 = 14	→	14 ÷ 2 = 7
8 × 2 = 16	→	16 ÷ 2 = 8
9 × 2 = 18	→	18 ÷ 2 = 9
10 × 2 = 20	→	20 ÷ 2 = 10
11 × 2 = 22	→	22 ÷ 2 = 11
12 × 2 = 24	→	24 ÷ 2 = 12

1. Write down the following division sums with the correct answers:

a. **4 ÷ 2 =**

b. **6 ÷ 2 =**

c. **2 ÷ 2 =**

d. **10 ÷ 2 =**

e. **8 ÷ 2 =**

f. $12 \div 2 =$

g. $22 \div 2 =$

h. $24 \div 2 =$

i. $18 \div 2 =$

j. $14 \div 2 =$

2. **Now answer the following questions:**

a. **Pogo has 4 children and he wants to give them some of his delicious red apples from his garden. He picks 8 apples altogether. If each child receives the same number of apples, how many apples will each child receive?**

b. **Pandora hides some of her toys in boxes. She decides to put 2 toys in each box. How many boxes will she need if she hides 12 toy soldiers?**

c. **If a teacher wants to divide 16 pencils into 2 equal lots, how many pencils will there be in each lot?**

d. **Zenda has to pack 2 suitcases with 14 shirts. If she wants to pack the same number of shirts into each suitcase, how many shirts will each suitcase contain?**

e. **Aunty Fifi wants to share a large cake with her family of 10. If she cuts the cake into 20 slices, how many slices of cake does each person receive?**

f. **Anton has to tidy up 24 pencils. He puts the same number of pencils in each of his 2 pencil cases. How many pencils will there be in each pencil case?**

g. **Billy is collecting all the tennis balls from the tennis court. He finds 18 tennis balls and he only has 2 bags to put them in. If he puts the same number of tennis balls into each bag, how many tennis balls will there be in each bag?**

h. Bindu takes 16 children to the park and she asks them to stand in pairs. How many pairs of children are there?

i. Alana finds 22 socks under her bed. How many pairs of socks is that?

j. Beth has 22 pairs of shoes that are too small for her. However, they fit her twin sisters perfectly. If she gives each of her twin sisters the same number of shoes, how many pairs of shoes will each twin sister receive?

3. **Copy out the following sums and put the correct number in the empty box:**

a. $10 \div \square = 1 \times 5$

b. $8 \div 2 = 2 \times \square$

c. $\square \div 2 = 3 \times 2$

d. $40 \div 5 = \square \times 2$

e. $60 \div \square = 10 + 2$

f. $\boxed{} \div 5 = 1 \times 2$

g. $40 \div \boxed{} = 6 - 2$

h. $120 \div 10 = 22 - \boxed{}$

i. $12 \times \boxed{} = 10 \times 6$

j. $\boxed{} \div 10 = 50 \div 5$

THE NUMBERS FAMILY

The Numbers family is a very large one. There are so many relatives that they cannot fit in the world and are scattered throughout the universe. So, there are Numbers everywhere. The most important members of the Numbers family are Mr Addition, Miss Subtraction, Mr Multiplication and Mrs Division.

Now Mr Addition is a very fat fellow with a wobbly chin and a smile as big as the new moon. His eyes twinkle like the stars because he keeps on finding new stars to add to the old ones. As he adds one number to another, his answers roll out like his laughter and his belly wobbles like jelly on a spoon.

Miss Subtraction is a very flighty young lady. She is forever losing things. She loses her clothes, her shoes, handbags, money, keys and she always loses her umbrella whenever she takes it out in the rain. She leaves behind her a trail of lost property. The problem is that she loves to subtract so much that she always ends up with less than she started with. Because she never has enough, she is always borrowing, especially from her next door neighbour. Fortunately, her friendly neighbour never grows angry with her because she is so pretty and always smiles when she borrows from him.

Mr Multiplication is altogether another story. In his big woolly jumper and soft shoes, he looks like a koala bear. He never stops complaining when Mr Addition goes round adding the stars. "Much better", says Mr

Multiplication, "to arrange everything into groups and multiply them instead." But Mr Addition refuses to change and says that there is enough room in the universe for both of them.

Mrs Division is very bossy. She is always organizing the members of the Numbers family. Although she loves Mr Multiplication very much, she always does the opposite to him. When he multiplies, she divides. She says that division is just as exciting as multiplication. Once she took a very large piece of paper and cut it into half. Now she had two pieces of paper. Then she cut each piece of paper into half again so that she had four pieces of paper. She enjoyed herself so much that she kept on folding and cutting all the pieces of paper into halves again and again. Eventually, she had sixty-four pieces of paper! She would have continued but the pieces of paper were now too small to fold!

Everyone in the Numbers family loves Grandpa, who is known as Grandpa Equals. Nothing pleases Grandpa Equals more than to see his nieces and nephews sitting on the old see-saw in the garden. Whenever the see-saw tilts upwards, he tells one of his nieces to climb on so that it is heavier. Whenever the see-saw tilts downwards, he tells one of his nephews to jump off so that it is lighter. Always, Grandpa Equals arranges his nieces and nephews so that the see-saw is perfectly level with the ground, so that neither one side is higher or lower than the other.

Two of Grandpa Equals' closest friends are Aunty Bigger and Aunty Smaller. Aunty Bigger is a very fat and very jolly woman who loves to cook. The trouble is that whenever she cooks something she never follows the instructions. She just can't help doubling everything: if the recipe says six eggs, she adds twelve. If you have to put in one bottle of milk, she puts in two. No wonder she is so wonderfully fat!

Her sister, Aunty Smaller, is quite different. She is ever so skinny with short bobbed hair, tiny hands and feet and she doesn't like anything that is too big, too noisy or more than it should be. Whatever her sister doubles, she halves. If six eggs are needed for a cake, she only puts in three; if one bottle of milk is the correct amount, she only pours in half a bottle of milk.

In particular, Aunty Bigger and Aunty Smaller love to relax on the see-saw. The trouble is that they can never get it to balance. Aunty Bigger's side of the see-saw always goes down and Aunty Smaller's side goes up into the air. Sometimes Grandpa Equals gets quite angry while the two Aunties giggle and bob up and down on the see-saw.

The Numbers family started hundreds and hundreds of years ago. The first ancestor recorded in history had the lovely name of Eternity. She was a star. Everyone loved her and everyone wanted to be just like her. Late at night when the sky is very dark, you can see her with all the other stars, twinkling and smiling at the rest of the world.

❧ LESSON **FORTY-SIX** ❧

A REVISION CHAPTER

1. **Add the following, setting out each sum in columns:**

    a. **49 + 15 =**

    b. **57 + 27 =**

    c. **123 + 398 =**

    d. **654 + 177 =**

    e. **801 + 119 =**

    f. **256 + 365 =**

    g. **468 + 357 =**

    h. **555 + 444 =**

    i. **702 + 27 =**

    j. **799 + 199 =**

2. **Subtract the following, setting out each sum in columns:**

  a. **65 − 4 =**

  b. **65 − 7 =**

  c. **281 − 127 =**

  d. **303 − 129 =**

  e. **512 − 326 =**

  f. **923 − 239 =**

  g. **604 − 418 =**

  h. **912 − 723 =**

  i. **650 − 153 =**

  j. **740 − 426 =**

3. **Multiply the following:**

  a. **5 × 5 =**

  b. **2 × 5 =**

  c. **10 × 2 =**

  d. **8 × 2 =**

e. **9 × 10 =**

f. **7 × 2 =**

g. **7 × 5 =**

h. **3 × 5 =**

i. **3 × 2 =**

j. **10 × 2 =**

k. **6 × 5 =**

l. **4 × 10 =**

m. **4 × 2 =**

n. **9 × 2 =**

o. **4 × 5 =**

p. **11 × 2 =**

q. **12 × 5 =**

r. **12 × 10 =**

s. **12 × 2 =**

t. **10 × 10 =**

4. Divide the following:

a. $5 \div 5 =$

b. $10 \div 5 =$

c. $10 \div 2 =$

d. $16 \div 2 =$

e. $20 \div 2 =$

f. $20 \div 10 =$

g. $20 \div 5 =$

h. $60 \div 10 =$

i. $30 \div 5 =$

j. $40 \div 5 =$

k. $100 \div 10 =$

l. $70 \div 10 =$

m. $14 \div 2 =$

n. $24 \div 2 =$

o. $35 \div 5 =$

p. $12 \div 2 =$

q. **4 ÷ 2 =**

r. **120 ÷ 10 =**

s. **10 ÷ 10 =**

t. **110 ÷ 10 =**

5. **Add the smallest number to the largest number:**

a. **27, 72, 83, 93, 29, 26**

b. **45, 54, 34, 43, 89, 98**

c. **111, 333, 222, 444, 555**

d. **765, 234, 123, 233, 332**

e. **201, 211, 173, 170, 168**

6. **Subtract the smallest number from the largest number:**

a. **27, 72, 25, 52, 71**

b. **55, 66, 44, 33, 22**

c. **121, 211, 201, 101, 102**

d. **468, 864, 246, 642, 579**

e. **615, 903, 839, 165, 195**

SOME UNUSUAL PROBLEMS

On a planet called Marzipo birthdays happen every 5 years, not every year as we are used to. Everyone in Marzipo has the family name of Marzipo.

1. If Jo Marzipo is 50 years old on our planet, how old is he in Marzipo?

2. Zimba Marzipo is four years old in Marzipo, how old is she where you live?

3. Lotte Marzipo is 12 years old in Marzipo time. How old is she in Earth time?

4. When Zig was 15 years old in Marzipo, his best friend Zog left Marzipo to live in England. In

Marzipo the sum of Zig's age and Zog's age was 25. How old was Zog in Earth time?

5. If you lived in Marzipo, how old would you be?

In Marzipo there are five meals a day, not three times a day as we are used to. There are no weekends in Marzipo either so that there are only 5 days in a week.

1. How many meals does a Marzipo eat in 1 week?

2. Zika Marzipo was ill for 3 weeks and did not eat anything at all. How many meals did Zika miss?

3. Apart from the first meal of the day, Wally Marzipo ends every meal with a biscuit. Before he goes to bed, Wally eats an extra biscuit. How many biscuits does he eat in a Marzipo week?

4. There are only 20 hours in a day in the land of Marzipo. Marinda Marzipo believes that meals should be spread out with exactly the same amount of time between each meal. In Marinda's home, therefore, how many hours are there between meals?

5. If you lived in Marzipo, how many more meals would you have in a week than you have on earth?

❧ LESSON **FORTY-SEVEN** ❧

Introduce the number **1000**. It is denoted by one set of thousands written as **1** in the thousands column, no sets of hundreds written as **0** in the hundreds column, no sets of tens written as **0** in the tens column and no sets of units written as **0** in the units column.

EXAMPLES:

$$
\begin{array}{r}
938 \\
+294 \\
\hline
1232 \\
\hline
\end{array}
$$

1 1 (carried over)

$$
\begin{array}{r}
1456 \\
+367 \\
\hline
1823 \\
\hline
\end{array}
$$

1 1 (carried over)

Note: the more advanced child may now grasp the range of numbers that becomes available simply by combining the digits **1** to **9** in the units, tens, hundreds and thousands column.

1. **Read aloud the following 4-digit numbers:**

    1001, 1010, 1100, 1101, 1110

    1909, 1900, 1190, 1009, 1999

    1700, 1077, 1770, 1707, 1117

2. **Write down the following numbers:**

    a. **one hundred and two**

    b. **one thousand and twenty**

239

c.   one thousand and ten

d.   eight hundred and eighty

e.   one thousand and eighty

f.   eleven

g.   one hundred and eleven

h.   one thousand and eleven

3. **Add the following:**

TAKE CARE TO WRITE EACH NUMERAL IN THE CORRECT COLUMN

a.   1019
     +891
     ‾‾‾‾

b.   1789
     +189
     ‾‾‾‾

c.   404
      +49
     ‾‾‾‾

d.   909
     +191
     ‾‾‾‾

e.   55
     +954
     ‾‾‾‾

f.   606
      +98
     ‾‾‾‾

g.
```
     707
     199
  +1189
  _____

  _____
```

h.
```
      89
     185
  +1285
  _____

  _____
```

i.
```
    1203
     891
   + 16
  _____

  _____
```

j.
```
    1899
   +111
  _____

  _____
```

4. **Write down the following sums in columns and work out the correct answers:**

   a. **606 + 44 + 1080 =**

   b. **88 + 808 + 214 =**

   c. **1000 + 10 + 100 =**

   d. **73 + 37 + 1001 =**

   e. **1000 + 99 + 101 =**

   f. **1000 + 303 + 97 =**

   g. **505 + 65 + 500 =**

h. **888 + 222 =**

i. **707 + 93 + 200 =**

j. **18 + 81 + 911 =**

5. **Now do these:**

a. **A bookshop sold 380 picture books, 200 story books and 156 cook books. How many books did it sell altogether?**

b. **Toby sells flower pots. On Monday he sold 81 flower pots, on Tuesday he sold 32 flower pots and on Wednesday he sold 10 flower pots. How many flower pots did he sell altogether on these three days?**

c. **Tonga sold soft ice-cream. She sold 420 scoops of ice-cream on Saturday and 1244 scoops of ice-cream on Sunday. How many scoops of ice-cream did Tonga sell altogether?**

d. **It was raining when Zak looked**

out of the window. He counted 64 umbrellas. A little later he counted 85 more umbrellas. When he looked out of the window a third time, he saw 38 umbrellas. How many umbrellas did Zak see altogether?

e. Frank went to the beach to collect shiny pebbles. He collected 329 of them. Later on, he found another 486. Finally, he added another 240 pebbles to his collection. How many pebbles did Frank have altogether?

f. Pongo loved to draw so he drew 89 green squares, 69 red squares and 48 yellow squares. How many squares did he draw altogether?

g. Some exercise books have 48 pages, some have 64 pages and some have only 24 pages. If I add these pages together, how many are there?

h. Farmer Zog planted 124 fir trees. He planted another 98 fir trees and then decided to plant 50 fir trees more. How many fir trees did he plant altogether?

i. Bobo delivered newspapers. He delivered 606 newspapers last week, 330 newspapers this week and tomorrow he has to deliver 64 newspapers. How many newspapers will he have delivered altogether?

j. Mum read a book that was 764 pages long. Dad read a book that was 646 pages long and Mili read a book that was only 64 pages long. How many pages did Mum, Dad and Mili read altogether?

6. Put the following numbers in order from the smallest to the largest:

111, 1011, 101, 1101, 1110

7. Put the following numbers in order from the largest to the smallest:

303, 4030, 4303, 4340, 4343, 403

PONTI PANDA GAZES AT THE STARS

Long ago, before numbers were known, there lived a tribe of people who could only count to two. A man was number one, his wife was number two. Everyone else was many: many children and many friends, many sheep and many cows, many trees and many flowers and many stars in the sky. Whenever the people of this tribe saw more than two, they saw many!

Before he knew about numbers, Ponti Panda was exactly the same. He was one bear, his reflection in the water was another bear and everyone else was many. On his birthday, he counted one present, then another present, and after that many presents.

But when Ponti Panda started to learn about numbers, everything changed. Instead of one birthday present, two birthday presents and many birthday presents, he discovered that sometimes he got ten birthday presents, sometimes fifteen birthday presents, and a few years ago on his best ever birthday

his friends gave him forty-two presents! Forty-two birthday presents sounded so much better than many birthday presents!

Every day Ponti Panda ate bamboo shoots. He loved bamboo shoots more than anything else. Sometimes he ate lots and lots of them. Before he could count, he never knew how many bamboo shoots he had eaten. When he ate ten, twenty or fifty bamboo shoots, he only knew that he had eaten many. But now he could tell the difference between twenty bamboo shoots and thirty bamboo shoots. When he grew too fat, he went on a diet and made sure that he never ate more than one hundred bamboo shoots in a single day!

However, Ponti Panda was still puzzled by the stars in the sky. Even with all the numbers that he had learned, he still couldn't count all of them. There were too many. There were more than a thousand. His friend, Wise Owl, who knew everything, told him about numbers that were so big that Ponti Panda couldn't even imagine that many bamboo shoots! More than anything, Ponti Panda wanted to keep on counting so that he could give everything he saw a number, which he thought was much better than just saying, "Many".